THE BEST OF SEASONS *Menu* COOKBOOK

JUDY *by* SCHULTZ

Food Styling by John Butler
Photography by Stephe Tate

The Publishers
Red Deer College Press
56 Avenue & 32 Street Box 5005 Red Deer Alberta Canada T4N 5H5

Food Styling by John Butler, Goldcay Food Stylist
Photography by Stephe Tate, Darklight Studios
Author Photo by Steve Makris
Design & Typography by Boldface Technologies Inc.
Illustrations by Delta Embree, Boldface Technologies Inc.
Printed & Bound in Singapore by Kyodo Printing Co. Pte. Ltd.

Special thanks to Patricia Roy for her assistance in the preparation of this book.

Special thanks to *The Edmonton Journal* and Radio 7 CKRD.

Special thanks to the following for contributing props for photography: cover: The Glasshouse (glassware); page 20: Polly Magoo's Ltée. (moroccan rug), Bernie Smith (mahogany plates), Mr. & Mrs. Birkbeck (spoons & basket); page 38: Allison Fuller (drapes & kitchen crockery); page 52: Campers Village (tackle box, camping set); page 102: The Artworks (Michael Graves coffee service), Ashbrooks (bed linen); page 130: The Wine Cask (wine barrel & bottles); page 152: Woodward's (plate setting); all fresh flowers courtesy of Holes Greenhouse. Photo assistant: Kathy Badger

Canadian Cataloguing in Publication Data
Schultz, Judy.
The best of seasons menu cookbook
ISBN 0-88995-065-2
1. Cookery   2. Menus.   I. Title
TX715.6.S38   1991   641.5   C90-091757-1

CONTENTS

INTRODUCTION

For me, food and its preparation have always been an adventure. Food is also, invariably, a sort of celebration.

My best and happiest times have always been when the people I love most are gathered around my table, and I can feed them until they holler for mercy but still go back for more.

In this, the second *Best of Seasons*, I've tied some of my favorite recipes to those seasonal feasts I love so much and to a few occasions that know no season – surviving the coldest month of winter, falling in love, getting married.

As in the first book, I owe my inspiration to the good cooks among my family, friends, and the many readers who have shared their culinary talents with me over the years. I thank them.

I owe special thanks this time to my friend, fellow food lover and colleague, Satya Das, one of Canada's finest wine writers.

Lies My Cookbook Told Me

Dear New Year, I hereby resolve to be wary of celebrity chefs who dash off cookbooks in idle moments. Yours truly, Judy.

That's it – my only resolution.

Here's why. In November, I bought a cookbook by that famous jet-everywhere Chef, Pomme D. Terre. His book, *Haute Cuisine Made Dead Easy*, was a smash hit, but he led me down the garden path, and I think I have a right to snivel.

After all, I trusted Chef Terre, whose face has long decorated magazines, cookbooks and commemorative coffee mugs. He's a man of the people. It says so right on the cover blurb. Having cooked his way through the social registers of major cities, he leaves behind a trail of personal endorsements from ecstatic hostesses.

"Pommy's *chou tête avec chapeau* was to die! It was utter heaven, just too divine! Ooh!" commented Ms. Julep Q. Porkeroll II, leading hostess of Dallas, Toronto, London and so forth.

Chef Terre holds occasional cooking classes, during which he sells autographed cookbooks and shares with his students such astute culinary observations as, "Cooking pasta is like making love," and "Peeling onions is like making love." And who can forget his truly insightful and often quoted maxim, "Cleaning fish is like making love."

Broiled Feta with Herbs

Tapenade of Roasted Peppers and Sun-Dried Tomatoes

Red Onion Focaccia with Poppyseeds

Winter Greens with Mushrooms and Grana

Three-Bean Cassoulet

Mom's Potato Casserole with Cheese and Cream

Butter Pecan Shortcake with Ice Cream and Hot Butterscotch Sauce

So I plunked down $59.95 for my personal copy, only to find after the second recipe (and we're already on page 47, snore) that Chef Terre can't be trusted.

His instructions are impossible to follow. His ingredients are impossible to find. And the results are iffy. I don't know what he had going with Ms. Julep, but I'll bet her maid did the cooking.

What follows is a sample of Chef Terre's culinary pipe dreams, with my advice to any unfortunate reader floundering through such a cookbook.

MAKE MEAT STOCK BY SIMMERING BONES 15 HOURS... Throw that book out, now! Anybody who has 15 spare hours to spend simmering bones is suffering from terminal boredom. Next you'll be cleaning your own chickens.

SEE PAGE FOUR OF RECIPE... Page four? He's kidding, right? No recipe should occupy that much space in a cookbook. After page one, maybe two, I'm outta here.

HAVE YOUR POULTERER DRAW THE SINEWS... Oh, to have a poulterer, let alone one who will draw the sinews. True, there may be the odd skilled poulterer hidden away in a posh part of town, but his number is unlisted, and his fortunate customers leave such information to favorite offspring in wills. The rest of us buy our chickens in plastic bags and deal with sinews later.

ASK YOUR FISHMONGER TO SKIN THE EEL... Fishmonger? What is that? The woman with the long red fingernails who sells me the odd halibut steak and a few crustaceans does not skin eels, she's not crazy about fileting sole and if I called her a fishmonger she'd hit me.

HAVE YOUR CHEESEMONGER PROVIDE A SAMPLE OF HIS BEST TRIPLE CREME... Here we go a-mongering again. Hard enough to find a triple creme, but samples? Dream on.

MAKE THE PUFF PASTRY... Right. And after you've spent eight hours making Chef Terre's puff pastry from scratch, he'll have you catch, pluck and draw three

Muscovy ducks for soup. This, when you can buy perfectly adequate puff pastry from frozen foodmongers.

ASK YOUR LOCAL GREENGROCER FOR HIS FINEST CHERVIL... At this moment, my local greengrocer is vacationing under a banana tree somewhere, and the kids he left in charge are having food fights with the tomatoes. The fuzzy-cheeked boy who bashes the lettuce around wouldn't know chervil from quack grass.

THIS ITEM IS AVAILABLE AT ANY GOOD SPECIALTY COUNTER... Oh, yeah? Well, I know six or ten specialty counters that have never even heard of it, much less stock the stuff.

And so it goes.

One of his monumental culinary lies deals with that great winter party dish from southwest France, cassoulet. Cassoulet is a savory, friendly mixture of beans and birds, perfect for a January party, and if you follow Pommy's instructions it might be ready by Easter. If you start now.

His version is from a specific village, involves 37 ingredients and sprawls over five pages. If he saw mine, he'd probably have a coronary – it's from nowhere in particular, breaks all conventions about the beans and birds, and it's the world's only nonlamb cassoulet.

I like to start this winter meal with strong, gutsy flavors in the appetizers. Serve cassoulet, potatoes and salad at the same time. It's less work, and the contrast in flavor and texture is perfect. The focaccia is a great bread to serve with this salad, and it goes well with the cassoulet too. The whole thing works together as a buffet, and the potatoes and cassoulet are even better made the day before.

BROILED FETA WITH HERBS

The sharp, salty flavor of good feta cheese, gentled with cream cheese and seasoned with dillweed, is a delicious combination. Try to find bulk feta – Greek or Italian markets have it, and it's milder than the tinned version. Fresh herbs are available year round in many markets, but dried herbs work well in this dish.

1 1/2 cups	feta cheese	375 mL
1 cup	cream cheese	250 mL
	juice of 1 lemon	
2 tsp	dillweed	10 mL
1/2 tsp	oregano	2 mL
2	garlic cloves, minced	2
	salt and freshly ground pepper	
	fresh dillweed or finely diced green onion top for garnish	
10	mini pitas	10

❖ Mash cheeses, lemon juice and spices together. Allow mixture to rest at room temperature about 30 minutes so flavors can mellow. Store, covered, in fridge until ready to use.

Spread generously on mini pitas. Broil until top begins to fleck golden brown. Serve hot, garnished with wisps of fresh dillweed or finely diced green onion top.

Serves 8 to 10.

TAPENADE OF ROASTED PEPPERS AND SUN-DRIED TOMATOES

A variation on the famous olive paste of southern Europe, this colorful, aromatic spread was one I first tasted in a kitchen in Calgary, Alberta. Buy dry-pack sun-dried tomatoes. Once they've been soaked, the flavor will be just as good as oil-pack, and they'll cost half as much. Primo and Unico both pack a good version of roasted sweet peppers, and they're so much easier than roasting your own.

1/2 cup	sun-dried tomatoes	125 mL
1 tbsp	olive oil	15 mL
2	cloves garlic, minced	2 cloves
1	medium onion, chopped	1
11 oz	jar roasted sweet peppers, drained	313 mL
2	ripe tomatoes, peeled and chopped	2
1 tbsp	balsamic vinegar	15 mL
1/2 tsp	sugar	2 mL
1 tsp	oregano	5 mL
	salt and black pepper	
3/4 cup	ripe olives, chopped	175 mL
1/2 cup	fresh parsley, chopped	125 mL
	sliced, toasted baguette	

❖ Cover sun-dried tomatoes with boiling water. Let steep for 2 hours until plumped up nicely. Drain any water that remains, as it will help remove excess salt. Leftovers should be covered with good olive oil and refrigerated for casual pizzas.

To make tapenade, heat oil in a frying pan, add garlic, onion, sweet peppers and sun-dried tomatoes. Cook about 1 minute at medium heat, making sure the garlic doesn't brown. (Scorched garlic is extremely bitter.)

Add ripe tomatoes, vinegar, sugar and seasonings. Simmer, stirring frequently, until most of the juice has evaporated. Cool slightly.

continues…

On the Table

This is a casual kitcheny meal to share with good friends. For a seated dinner, arrange small terra cotta pots of green herbs or healthy houseplants with plain white candles on a wooden table. Red place mats, or something homespun, will be a smashing complement. If it's a buffet, fill a big oblong basket with gorgeous vegetables – red, yellow and green peppers, a bosomy purple eggplant, a fennel bulb. Tuck in heads of garlic and a few banana peppers for contrast. Don't forget the candles.

Purée the mixture coarsely, using either a food processor or blender. Stir in olives and taste for seasoning. Store in a covered container overnight to allow flavors to ripen. Just before serving, add chopped parsley.

To serve, pile the tapenade generously on toasted baguette slices. Serves 8 to 10.

COOK'S NOTE: This will keep, covered and refrigerated, about a week, or frozen for three months.

If you'd like to roast your own peppers, grill them until the skin chars and blisters, then peel.

To toast the baguette, slice diagonally into 1/2 inch (1 cm) thick slices. Brush lightly on both sides with olive oil. Arrange on a baking sheet and broil until barely browned. Turn and broil other side. The toast is served cold, so it may be made well ahead of time.

RED ONION FOCACCIA WITH POPPYSEEDS

This recipe, adapted from a Fleichmann's pizza recipe, produces a wonderfully chewy flatbread at lightning speed. Serve it with the main course as a bread to complement the crisp greens in the salad.

FLATBREAD

1	envelope quick-rise instant yeast	1
2 1/2 cups	all-purpose flour	625 mL
1 tsp	salt	5 mL
1/2 tsp	oregano	2 mL
1 cup	water	250 mL
1/4 cup	olive oil	50 mL

❖ Preheat oven to 450 F (230 C).

Reserve 1 cup (250 mL) flour from total amount. Mix remaining flour, salt, oregano and yeast in a large bowl.

Heat water and oil until hot to touch, 125 – 130 F (50 – 55 C). Stir hot liquids into seasoned flour mixture.

Stir in enough reserved flour to make a soft dough that does not stick to the bowl. Turn out onto a floured board and knead until smooth and elastic, about 5 minutes. Cover and let rest 10 minutes. Cut dough in half and roll each piece to fit a 12 inch (30 cm) pizza pan. Fit each piece into a pizza pan, pushing it up the sides. Spread with red onion topping.

TOPPING

3	red onions, chopped	3
1 tbsp	olive oil	15 mL
3 tbsp	butter	45 mL
2 tbsp	poppy seeds	30 mL

❖ Over medium heat, in a large frying pan, sauté onions in butter and oil until transparent. Do not brown.

Divide onions and melted butter-oil mixture between the two flatbreads, spreading evenly over the surface. Pat down gently with a spatula. Sprinkle poppy seeds over each flatbread. Bake 20 minutes or until done.

To serve, slice into wedges and arrange on a napkin-lined tray. Serves 10 generously.

WINTER GREENS WITH MUSHROOMS AND GRANA

Be sure to use freshly grated cheese here – Parmesan, Romano or aged Asiago. Any good Italian grating cheese will do. Prepackaged cheese dust won't.

1	head romaine lettuce	1
1	bunch fresh spinach	1
2 cups	white mushrooms, sliced	500 mL
1/2 cup	Parmesan, Romano or aged Asiago, grated	125 mL
	freshly ground black pepper	
1/4 cup	red wine vinegar	50 mL
1/2 cup	canola oil	125 mL
1/2 tsp	dry mustard	2 mL
1	clove garlic, mashed	1 clove
1 tsp	salt	5 mL
1 cup	cheese croutons	250 mL
3	slices bacon, cooked crisp	3

❖ Tear washed romaine and spinach leaves into a large glass bowl. Toss sliced mushrooms over top. Sprinkle with grated cheese and a generous grinding of black pepper. Place vinegar, oil, dry mustard, garlic and salt in a blender and process briefly. Pour over salad. Sprinkle with croutons and crumbled bacon. Toss and serve. Serves 8 to 10.

THREE BEAN CASSOULET

A big-hearted dish, full of earthy, wintery flavors. It will feed everybody and still leave a bean or two for the dog. Don't let the lengthy ingredient list scare you – it goes together quickly and is worth the effort.

1	slice bacon, diced	1
4	chicken legs	4
1	small duck	1
1 lb	garlic sausage	500 g
3	cloves garlic, minced	3
1	large onion, chopped	1
1	stalk celery, chopped	1
2	carrots, chopped	2
1	28 oz (796 mL) can tomatoes	1
1 cup	red wine	250 mL
1 cup	beef bouillon	250 mL
1/2 tsp	ground cloves	2 mL
1 tsp each	cinnamon and thyme	5 mL
1	large bay leaf	1
1	19 oz (540 mL) can chickpeas, drained	1
1	19 oz (540 mL) can kidney beans, drained	1
1	19 oz (540 mL) can beans with pork	1
	salt and pepper	
2 cups	bread crumbs	500 mL
1/2 cup	fresh parsley, chopped	125 mL
	olive oil	

continues…

In the Bottle

Forthright appetizer flavors

demand robust wine. Chilled

Boutari, a sturdy Greek wine,

stands up to feta and peppers.

For a simpler counterpoint,

try Toscano Bianco from a

major house. Tavel rosé is also

a fine start – firm, even

astringent, it may even stand

up to cassoulet and can last

through dinner. Rhone red is a

must with cassoulet. A ripe

Gigondas at least seven or

eight years old cuts through…

❖ Preheat oven to 350 F (180 C).

In a heavy Dutch oven, fry the bacon. Pat chicken pieces dry and brown in bacon fat, adding a drop of oil if necessary. Remove and reserve. Cut duck into pieces. Brown in the same pot. Remove and reserve.

Cut garlic sausage into generous chunks. Brown quickly.

Add garlic, onion, celery and carrots, and continue cooking over medium heat until onions are soft.

Add tomatoes, red wine, beef bouillon, spices and bay leaf.

Return bird parts to the pan. Turn up heat to simmer, reduce heat and cover the pot. Cook over low heat about 1 hour.

Remove bay leaf. Add all beans to the pot, stirring lightly to distribute everything. If mixture seems dry, add a little water. Season with salt and pepper.

Mix bread crumbs and parsley, and sprinkle over top of mixture, patting gently. Drizzle lightly with olive oil.

Bake 40 minutes. Stir the crust down into the mixture and continue baking another 20 minutes. Serves 8 to 10.

MOM'S POTATO CASSEROLE WITH CHEESE AND CREAM

In January, a pot of soft, creamy mashed potatoes is infinitely comforting, and it will balance all the assertive flavors in this cold weather menu.

8	large potatoes	8
1	8 oz (250 g) pkg light cream cheese, mashed	1
1/2 cup	yogurt	125 mL
2 tbsp	butter	30 mL
2 tbsp	mayonnaise	30 mL
2	green onions, minced	2
1 cup	Cheddar cheese, grated	250 mL
	salt and pepper	
1	egg, beaten	1

❖ Preheat oven to 375 F (190 C).

Peel and boil potatoes until fork-tender. Drain and mash. Add cream cheese, yogurt, butter and onion. Whip until smooth and soft. Stir in Cheddar cheese, salt, pepper and beaten egg. Scoop into a 2 qt (2 L) casserole.

Bake about 30 minutes or until lightly browned. Serves 8 to 10.

…the earthy taste of beans. A Cornas of similar age is fine, as is a premium St. Joseph red like Chapoutier's Deschants or Jaboulet's La Grande Pompée. Côte-Rôtie and Hermitage are too high flown for comfort food like cassoulet, but if you have the means, indulge. Fortified wine can be paired with butterscotch sauce. Unusual though it may sound, try a white port like Taylor's Chip Dry. That, or chilled marsala.

BUTTER PECAN SHORTCAKE WITH ICE CREAM AND HOT BUTTERSCOTCH SAUCE

An old-fashioned dessert with warm, butternut flavors.

2 cups	all-purpose flour	500 mL
1/4 cup	brown sugar	50 mL
3 tsp	baking powder	15 mL
1/2 tsp	salt	2 mL
1/2 cup	butter	125 mL
1/2 cup	pecans, chopped	125 mL
1	egg	1
3/4 to 1 cup	milk	175 to 250 mL
	butter pecan ice cream	

❖ Preheat oven to 400 F (200 C).

In a large bowl, mix together flour, sugar, baking powder and salt. Cut in butter until mixture resembles coarse crumbs. Stir in pecans.

Beat egg with a fork and add to mixture. Gradually add enough milk to form a dough, stirring lightly. (Too much milk will make the dough too soft to handle easily, too little will make it crumbly.) Turn dough onto a lightly floured surface and knead 5 or 6 times.

On an ungreased baking pan, pat dough into a round loaf roughly 9 inches (22 cm) in diameter. Brush top of dough with milk and sprinkle with sugar.

With a knife, mark loaf into 8 to 10 wedges. Bake 15 to 20 minutes, until golden brown. Let cool slightly before serving.

To serve, split cake horizontally, then cut into the marked wedges. Sandwich a scoop of butter pecan ice cream into each wedge. Drizzle with Hot Butterscotch Sauce. Serves 8 to 10.

COOK'S NOTE: If baking the shortcake doesn't fit your schedule, or if you'd prefer a lighter dessert, peel and slice 4 winter pears. Drop them in the Hot Butterscotch Sauce about two minutes, just to warm them, and serve with vanilla ice cream.

HOT BUTTERSCOTCH SAUCE

This is the sauce the cooks in my family have always served with winter desserts – shortcake, carrot pudding, sometimes plain white cake – always accompanied by a good smash of ice cream.

1 1/2	cups brown sugar	375 mL
2 tbsp	butter	30 mL
2 tbsp	cornstarch	30 mL
1 1/2 cups	cold water	375 mL
1 tsp	vanilla	5 mL

❖ Put sugar and butter in a medium saucepan and place over medium heat. Quickly dissolve cornstarch in cold water and add to sugar mixture. Cook over medium heat, stirring constantly, until thick and clear. Remove from heat and add vanilla. Makes about 2 cups (250 mL).

Paris When it Drizzled

I first tasted couscous in Morocco, back in the mid-70s, when little black-eyed boys sold hashish on street corners and the remnants of the flower-child generation still haunted the bazaar.

That couscous couldn't have been a memorable meal because I forgot it for about ten years. Then, one February, I ended up in Paris, camped for a while in the apartment of a chef who rented his digs to selected transients.

Camille, my friend and fellow transient, agreed to stock the bar, and I was in charge of the kitchen, which was mousehole small. If I stood exactly in the middle I could reach anything in the room: frying pans on the south wall, knife rack on the north, cupboard to the west (coffee, chocolate, olive oil in there), sink and two-burner stove to the east. The mini-fridge was never cold, the toy-sized oven was never hot, but it was Paris.

I wish I had done more cooking there, but we had many meals with various chefs, so there wasn't much need. For some reason, each chef chose to feed us duck. During one three-day marathon, we ate duck with olives, caramelized duck with orange and Rouenaise duck with apples. The chef explained gleefully that this particular duck had been strangled "...slowly, gently, so the blood will rush to the breast and give a new dimension of flavor. *Formidable!*"

Easy for you to say, I thought, but did anybody ask the duck? It put me off haute

Smoky Almonds with Olives

*Couscous with Peas and
Green Herbs*

*Grilled Eggplant, Zucchini
and Sweet Peppers*

*Chicken with
Sweet Onion Confit*

*Upside Down Apple Tart with
Red Grapes*

cuisine for weeks. Too full of rich food to think of duck *a la* anything, we turned to simpler fare.

The apartment was on the Ile de la Cité, a few steps from Notre-Dame and just a bridge away from the rue du Huchette, a short, touristy street of Middle Eastern and Moroccan restaurants.

Mainstream dining guides studiously ignored these restaurants, and when we quizzed a man who published a food and wine newsletter, he turned his nose up and said nobody actually ate there.

But I liked the Tunisian bakery with its honey-dripped pastries that exploded in a shower of rosewater when I bit into them, and Camille longed to dance to the wild bouzouki bands that played every night.

So one night we picked a restaurant where a lamb had been slowly turning on a spit in the front window since noon and a sign in the window said "Couscous." Good, I thought, no duck. The place seemed more Greek than Moroccan, but it was crowded and smelled good, and a bouzouki trio was strumming itself into a frenzy, so in we went, all the way to the back where there was nothing between us and the dancers but a lot of smashed crockery.

Two lithe Arab girls danced together, holding a scarf between them, a fat redhead in a tight yellow T-shirt waddled through some steps with surprising grace and a beautiful Greek girl sang, but not very well.

The best dancer was a tall, slim waiter who loved the music, loved smashing the plates and doing his dance with his own intricate steps. When he was pouring wine or bringing more bread he was just another waiter, but when he danced he was so sensual and intense that every woman in the room, and many of the men, got lost in his music.

The couscous was also memorable – fine grained semolina that had been hand-rolled for hours and hours, the dancing waiter explained. It was dribbled with the fiery sauce called *harissa*.

I make a simpler version with fast couscous, the kind that drives purists crazy but makes perfect sense for busy people who are fighting the February blahs.

The chicken can be prepared the day before, and the vegetables can be sliced and covered early in the day, ready when you are. Although it's traditionally lucky to serve seven vegetables with couscous, three are better for my schedule and my friends' appetites.

SMOKY ALMONDS WITH OLIVES

If your friends arrive early in the afternoon and look hungry, add cubes of good feta cheese, sprinkled with a little oregano, and a loaf of warm crusty bread. They can nibble happily until dinner is ready, hours from now. But if you plan to eat soon, stick with the almonds and olives.

The best olives are available in bulk at Italian or Greek markets. Buy small amounts of several kinds – salty purple Nicoise, green, meaty Picholines, the almond-shaped Kalamata and a few peppery Escabeche if you can find them.

1 tbsp	butter	15 mL
1 cup	Smokehouse almonds	250 mL
1 cup	blanched almonds	250 mL
3 to 4 drops	Tabasco sauce	3 to 4 drops
2 cups	oil-cured bulk olives, mixed	500 mL

❖ Melt butter in a heavy frying pan. Toss Smokehouse almonds and blanched almonds over medium heat until blanched nuts begin to color slightly. Add Tabasco and toss well. Turn off heat. Place hot nuts in one dish, olives in another and let guests help themselves. Provide small napkins for wiping fingers, as this simple appetizer is delicious but messy. Serves 8 to 10.

On the Table

Arrange a few mimosa sprigs in a jug with a branch of bittersweet or other small red berries. No berries? Have the mimosa alone or with a mix of white and yellow tulips and candles in an informal arrangement on a bare wooden table. Mix small votive candles with one or two big fat ones in wooden holders. Yellow napkins will be smashing.

Couscous with Peas and Green Herbs

Quick couscous is a handier version of the long-cooked kind. The texture is slightly different, but the end result is very good.

3 tbsp	butter	45 mL
2 cups	chicken stock	500 mL
1 1/2 cups	quick couscous	375 mL
1 cup	tiny green peas, frozen	250 mL
1	green onion, minced	1
1/4 cup	fresh parsley, minced	50 mL

❖ Melt butter in a medium saucepan, add chicken stock and bring to a boil. Run hot water over peas to thaw. Add couscous to stock and immediately turn heat off. Add peas and fluff with a fork. Cover and let stand 5 minutes. Add onion and parsley and toss. Mound on a platter and surround with grilled vegetables. Serves 8 to 10.

GRILLED EGGPLANT, ZUCCHINI AND SWEET PEPPERS

Take the time to presalt and drain the eggplant. It's good insurance against a bitter one, which pops up now and then no matter how plump and glossy it may look. In the interest of economy, you may want to substitute green peppers for yellow. Thick slices of red or sweet white onions also grill beautifully, but they're omitted here because of the onion confit.

1	medium eggplant	1
2	zucchini	2
2	red sweet peppers	2
2	yellow sweet peppers	2
1/2 cup	olive oil	125 mL
1 tbsp	red wine vinegar	15 mL
2 tbsp	soya sauce	30 mL
	salt and freshly ground pepper	
	cilantro leaves or green onion sprigs for garnish	

❖ Cut top and bottom off eggplant. Slice into 4 rounds. Cut each round in half. Lay slices on a plate and sprinkle with salt.

Slice zucchini in half lengthwise, then crosswise. Core and seed peppers. Cut each pepper in quarters.

Rinse and drain eggplant. Pat dry.

Pour oil, wine vinegar and soya sauce in a large shallow dish, coating the bottom well. Lay vegetable slices in marinade. Coat well and turn, making sure the marinade is well distributed on the vegetables. Cover and leave at room temperature for up to 1 hour or refrigerate until 1 hour before grilling. It may be necessary to brush vegetables with additional oil before grilling.

Place eggplant on an oiled grill and cook until golden. Add zucchini and peppers, skin-side down. Turn eggplant when it reaches a deep golden brown. Allow peppers to blister slightly before turning. Turn zucchini when flesh is golden. Continue grilling until vegetables are quite soft and eggplant is deep golden brown on both sides.

Sprinkle with salt and freshly ground pepper, and arrange around the mound of couscous. Garnish with fresh cilantro leaves, if available, or with sprigs of onion green. Serves 8.

COOK'S NOTE: Thanks to gas barbecues, we now grill all year round. But if you're an apartment dweller, or there's a blizzard howling, the oven broiler works just as well.

CHICKEN WITH SWEET ONION CONFIT

This is one of my favorite dishes for winter evenings. The robust spices, melting sweetness of the onions and the fat, juicy raisins are a perfect foil for a blizzard.

6	whole chicken breasts	6
1 tbsp	soft butter	15 mL
1/4 cup	liquid honey	50 mL
	salt and pepper	
6	large onions, peeled and sliced	6
1 tbsp	olive oil	15 mL
2 tbsp	butter	30 mL
	salt	
1/2 tsp each	ginger, cloves and thyme	2 mL each
1 tsp each	cinnamon and curry powder	5 mL each
1 tsp	mustard seed	5 m
3 tbsp	brown sugar	45 mL
2 cups	chicken stock	500 mL
1 cup	golden raisins	250 mL

❖ Preheat oven to 500 F (260 C).

Split chicken breasts along backbone, removing bone if you wish, but retaining skin. Place chicken breasts skin-side up in a baking pan. Stir butter and honey together and brush over chicken. Season lightly with salt and pepper. Bake chicken in a hot oven about 10 minutes. Reduce heat to 375 F (190 C), pour onion confit over chicken and continue baking about 30 minutes or until chicken is thoroughly cooked.

To make the confit, fry onions in oil and butter in a Dutch oven until they're transparent. (Don't let them brown.) Sprinkle with salt, spices and sugar. Cover and cook over low heat about 20 minutes. Add chicken stock and raisins and continue cooking until much of the juice has reduced and sauce has thickened. Reserve until you need it for the chicken.

Serve chicken on a large platter, drizzled with the sauce. Extra sauce may be served on the side. Serves 8 to 10.

UPSIDE DOWN APPLE TART WITH RED GRAPES

We have the old Tatin sisters to thank for this dessert. It's perfectly delicious made with apples alone, but I like the red Chilean grapes – they add oomph.

1/2	14.5 oz (411 g) pkg puff pastry	1/2
3 tbsp	unsalted butter	45 mL
1 cup	white sugar	250 mL
2 tsp	lemon rind, grated	10 mL
	juice of 1 lemon	
1/2 tsp	cinnamon	2 mL
1 cup	red Chilean grapes	250 mL
6	Granny Smith apples	6
2 tbsp	brown sugar	30 mL
	whipped cream (optional)	

❖ Remove puff pastry from freezer just long enough to thaw slightly. It must remain cold. Preheat oven to 400 F (200 C). Have a 10 inch (1 L) pie plate ready.

Melt butter in a medium saucepan. Add sugar, cinnamon, lemon juice and rind as soon as butter foams. Cook over medium heat until syrupy and beginning to color. Pour syrup in bottom of the pie plate. Sprinkle grapes in plate.

Peel, core and thickly slice apples. Arrange apple slices in concentric pattern over the grapes. Sprinkle with brown sugar.

Roll puff pastry into a circle slightly larger than the plate. Roll pastry onto rolling pin and place over apples, tucking it around them so they're snug. Cut two or three small slashes in the crust so steam can escape.

Place pie on a baking sheet in the center of oven. Bake 40 to 45 minutes or until crust is golden brown and juice has bubbled around the edge.

Let pie rest 5 minutes for juices to set. Run a sharp knife around the edge of the plate to loosen. To remove, invert a serving plate over the pie plate and flip over. Garnish with piped whipped cream if desired.

Serve warm, reheating if necessary. Serves 8.

Breakfast in Winter

*Orange Flower Tangerines
with Caramelized Lime*

———

*George's Porridge with Fruit,
Nuts and Seeds*

———

*Cheese-Stuffed French Toast
with Cherry Syrup*

———

Quick Pain Au Chocolat

———

Mixed Breakfast Grill

———

The Coffee Bar

W hen I cook simple things well, I feel wise and content, secure in the knowledge that I can survive, if I have to, with very little in the cupboard.

Porridge, for instance. Real, wintertime porridge. It's about as simple as food can ever be – a few grains of wheat or oats, flattened and cooked in plain water with a pinch of salt.

The smell of porridge cooking takes me back to the very edge of childhood mornings, with my long stockings warming behind the stove and my dog waiting patiently for me to award him the last bite from the bowl.

I find that dogs, who are discerning eaters anyhow, enjoy a good feed of porridge now and then. In the Saskatchewan village where I ate most of my porridge, a big old collie-type lived with us whenever he felt like it. We also had a regulation family dog who slept in the house, but the collie was essentially a free spirit. We named him George.

George was mostly black, with three white socks and a patch of white on his tail, as though his mother had shopped around for the right combination. If he'd been human, he could have lived well as a gigolo in any number of upscale watering holes. As it was, George was the sort of animal that makes strong men scratch their heads and ponder the wheel of life.

One spring after he'd had a brief romance with a comely mongrel, he decided to fight the entire canine population in celebration. It was nearly the end of him. George was found in a ditch near our house, gasping his last, so my parents loaded him on a blanket, turned it into a makeshift stretcher and lugged him home, where we all stood around checking his wounds.

One eye was swollen shut. An ear was bleeding. He had been bruised, bitten, gouged, scratched and generally whupped. He raised his head a little, gave one mournful groan, flopped back and looked dead. Naturally, I began to wail.

Grandma said hmpf, she'd seen worse, and maybe this would teach the old fool to behave himself. Then she prescribed a good dose of electric oil and a bowl of porridge, which was his favorite meal whenever he was in residence. We thinned the porridge with milk, in deference to his weakened condition, and in no time George was back on the road. As Grandma said, "My, my! That dog is sassier than ever!"

There's no definite recipe for porridge. Just mix rolled oats with Red River Cereal or Sunny Boy (anything with a few flax seeds and some cracked wheat), and follow the directions on the package. I like to mix two or three kinds together, cooking it all quite a long time, because porridge should not be served al dente. Throw in raisins, dried apple bits or sunflower seeds to give it more texture and snap.

The milk goes on first, then a dribble of cream right in the middle, followed by lashings of demarara sugar, the moist kind that goes rock hard about five seconds after you forget to close the bag. Start eating from the outer edge, where it's cooler, because digging into the middle is a sure way to burn your tongue.

Leftover porridge has been the subject of much discussion among foodies. A good Scottish cook told me about shepherds in the north of Scotland who love a slab of cold porridge for lunch. They whack off a lump in the morning, after it has congealed, stuff it in their pocket and away they go.

Grandma insisted that leftover porridge could be salted, peppered, onioned and fried for supper, but she never tried it on me. I was duly grateful. What you do with leftover porridge is your own business, but I would check with the dog before I started chopping the onions.

This is a big breakfast, the sort of meal that can stoke your appetite before a day of skiing, or take most of the morning to eat and then wander into the afternoon if you want it to. It's also infinitely flexible – if you end up with a crowd, just make more French toast and throw another sausage on the grill.

ORANGE FLOWER TANGERINES WITH CARAMELIZED LIME

Versions of this recipe can be found in Middle Eastern or North African cookbooks. Mine was adapted from one that appears in Paula Wolfert's wonderful book, *World Of Food*. Use clementines, tangerines or sweet mandarins for this, but avoid royal mandarins, which are riddled with seeds. Seedless navel oranges also work well here. Orange flower water is available from specialty food shops or Asian grocers. The best comes from France in a pretty blue bottle.

10 to 12	seedless tangerines	10 to 12
3 tbsp	orange flower water	45 mL
1/2 cup	liquid honey	125 mL
1/2 tsp	cinnamon	2 mL
3	large limes	3
3/4 cup	sugar	175 mL
3/4 cup	water	175 mL
	mint leaves for garnish (optional)	

❖ Peel oranges, removing as much of the white pithy membrane as possible. Slice into a large bowl.

Stir together orange flower water, liquid honey and cinnamon. Pour over oranges, cover closely with wax paper and refrigerate several hours.

Meanwhile, peel the zest (outside peel only) from limes with a vegetable peeler. With a sharp knife, cut into fine strips and place in a small saucepan. Cover with boiling water, boil 1 minute, drain and reserve. Reserve limes for another use.

Put sugar and water in a small saucepan. Bring to a boil and cook until it just begins to color slightly (caramelize). Add strips of lime peel, turn heat down and simmer about 3 minutes or until peel caramelizes. Pour onto a wax paper-lined tray until it dries, about 2 hours.

To serve, arrange the orange slices on a platter with a lip to hold the juices. Sprinkle the oranges with the caramelized lime peel. Garnish with mint leaves if available. Serves 8 to 10.

On the Table

Generously cover a round basket with florist's moss to make a bird's nest, weaving a few small dried silk flowers into it. Fill the nest with hard-boiled eggs. If Easter happens to fall in March, color the eggs. If you're serving buffet style, add a tall bouquet of pussy willows with daffodils.

GEORGE'S PORRIDGE WITH FRUIT, NUTS AND SEEDS

A satisfying, comforting, healthy start for an active winter day – try it, you'll like it. Use any favorite porridge cooked according to package directions, and keep it hot in a chafing dish or double boiler wrapped with a colorful tea towel.

hot porridge for 8
milk
cream
demarara sugar
raisins, dried apricots and dried apples (mixed together)
shelled sunflower seeds, chopped pecans and chopped almonds (mixed together)

❖   Let people help themselves to porridge directly from the pot (a big double boiler works best here).

Right beside the porridge pot, arrange all the fixin's – a bowl of raisins and dried fruit, a bowl of seeds and nuts, a big pitcher of milk, a smaller pitcher of cream and a bowl of demarara sugar.

CHEESE-STUFFED FRENCH TOAST WITH CHERRY SYRUP

If you're patient with this toast once it's in the oven, it puffs slightly and develops a wonderfully crisp exterior while the cheese turns to molten gold inside. It's almost as good with maple syrup as with cherry syrup.

8	slices French or Italian bread, 1 inch (2.5 cm) thick	8
8	slices Cheddar cheese, 1/4 inch (1/2 cm) thick	8
1 1/2 cups	milk	375 mL
6	eggs	6
3/4 cup	flour	175 mL
1/2 tsp	baking powder	2 mL
1/2 tsp	salt	2 mL
	butter	

❖ Preheat oven to 400 F (200 C).

Pour milk in a shallow dish. Beat together eggs, flour, baking powder and salt, and pour in another shallow dish.

Cut a deep slit in the side of each slice of bread. Stuff in a slice of Cheddar cheese, trimming it to fit. Dip each slice in milk, turning once, then in the batter, turning several times to coat thoroughly.

Melt butter in a large frying pan that has first been coated with a little oil. Quickly brown each slice on both sides. Transfer slices to a buttered baking sheet and bake about 20 minutes or until slightly puffed and golden. Serve at once with Cherry Syrup. Serves 8.

COOK'S NOTE: If you wish to gild the lily, dust the slices with icing sugar and cinnamon.

CHERRY SYRUP

If you love cinnamon, lemon, or both, a dash of cinnamon and a wisp of grated lemon peel won't hurt here, but it's fine the way it is.

1 cup	cherry jam	250 mL
1 tsp	cornstarch, dissolved	5 mL
1 cup	cherry juice	250 mL
1/2 cup	water	125 mL
2 cups	red sour pitted cherries, drained	500 mL

❖ In a small saucepan, melt cherry jam over low heat, stirring constantly. Stir cornstarch into a little cherry juice and then dissolve in remaining juice and water. Pour into melted jam and continue simmering, stirring constantly, until slightly thick and clear. Stir in cherries. Serve hot with French toast. Makes about 3 1/2 cups (875 mL).

QUICK PAIN AU CHOCOLAT

For a big breakfast like this, offer a second bread. These fast, chocolate-stuffed crescents are easy to do, and although a good French bakery is the preferred route, you'll find this to be a toothsome substitute.

1	8 oz (250 g) pkg refrigerated croissant dough	1
1 1/2 cups	milk chocolate, chopped	375 mL

❖ Preheat oven to 350 F (180 C).

Unroll croissant dough and separate into 8 triangles along perforations.

Divide chocolate bits (a chocolate bar, chopped, works well here) evenly among the triangles, spooning them into little piles on the widest end. Starting at the wide end, roll into crescents and place on an ungreased baking sheet.

Bake 10 minutes or until golden brown. Serve hot in a napkin-lined basket. Makes 8, so you may wish to double the recipe.

MIXED BREAKFAST GRILL

16	slices back bacon	16
16	slices lean side bacon	16
16	fresh pork sausages	16

❖ Preheat broiler.

Lay bacon slices on a cold broiler pan. Prick sausages and add to bacon, using a second pan if necessary.

Broil bacon, turning the side bacon several times if necessary. Remove to a paper-lined tray when done to taste. Keep warm. Continue cooking pork sausages until crisp and brown. Surround platter of French toast with bacon and sausages or serve them on a separate platter. Serves 8 to 10.

In the Bottle

There's really only one ideal with a breakfast like this – premium champagne. If you have Krug tastes and a normal budget, think of Domaine Chandon reserve. This rich biscuity wine is a baby Krug at a quarter the price. Drink it throughout, except with the chocolate. If you can afford it, go for a grande marque…

THE COFFEE BAR

❖ On a side table, arrange cups, spoons and two pots of coffee –
one regular, one decaf. Also offer a pot of hot milk for the au lait
crowd, a bowl of whipped cream, a small bowl of grated chocolate
and a bowl of coarse brown sugar. Let them help themselves to
coffee. That way they can have it either straight up or loaded, as
the whim strikes.

…Krug Grande Cuvée,
Taittinger Comtes de
Champagne, Billecart-Salmon
Blanc des Blancs or Rosé or a
Bollinger Recemment
Degorgé. Offer a tall pitcher
of fresh orange juice, or mix
orange and grapefruit for
those who must reluctantly
pass up the champagne.

The Garlic Woman and The Grand Aioli

Her name was Thérèse.

People in the village called her Old Thérèse because she was eightyish and because a younger Thérèse, who was only seventy-something, lived just down the road.

But I think of Thérèse as the Garlic Woman.

She lived on the north coast of Normandy, spit distance from Dieppe, but she was born in the south, near Nice. After so many years of cooking and gardening by one sea or another, she knew everything about food. She adored garlic, and every meal I ate with her was laced with it. In that way she was more Provençal than Norman.

"Never trust a man who doesn't love garlic. He has no courage. No soul. He will disappoint you in every way," the garlic woman told me darkly, as though from experience.

On a rainy night in early spring, we sat in her kitchen, eating one of her favorite things – winkles in cream, laced with so much garlic that the heady perfume filled the house from bottom to top and brought her grandchildren running for a taste. Another night she tottered down the stairs in gray lace and pearls, demanding restaurant pizza "with lots of garlic, *n'est-ce pas? Quoi?*"

We had one garlic disaster on a day when Old Thérèse had a cold that even regular

Tapenade Niçoise

Quick Grisini with Rosemary

Tea-Smoked Eggs

Aioli with Parsley

Boiled Shrimp

Oven-Baked Salmon

Cucumber-Dill Sauce with Mustard and Tarragon

Spring Vegetable Basket

Double Chocolate Carrot Cake with Brown Sugar Icing

libations of cognac failed to budge. Because of this, she put her little granddaughter and the Swedish *au pair* in charge of lunch.

The *au pair*, who was terrified of the coffee machine and had never managed a whole meal before, did the only logical thing – began chopping garlic. When she had enough to choke a horse, she sprinkled it over a few lettuce leaves and sloshed on a lot of vinegar (no oil, not a speck of salt). Old Thérèse tasted, chewed, choked, wiped her eyes. The sensitive *au pair* began to cry.

"Never mind, *chérie*, you'll marry a rich man, he'll hire a cook," cried Thérèse. We ate cheese and bread.

The next afternoon, her sister, Celeste, who was ninety-something, came to lunch and said she'd stay for dinner, so they decided to have a party.

"We'll have the *aioli*. *Le grande aioli*, like we made in the old days in the Luberon!" Oh Lord, I thought, more garlic. Spare me.

"But you will love it," yelled Celeste, who was a little deaf. "You have never tasted anything so good as our *aioli*! Never!"

For the next hour, a loud discussion raged, hinging upon the slovenly habits of various local cooks who couldn't make a decent mayonnaise, never mind the glorious garlic mayonnaise, their beloved *aioli*. Such people were everywhere and not to be trusted. Names were named, scandals raked up, reputations shredded. The two old girls fell around the room, cackling and gossiping, but eventually they started the *aioli*.

Between nips of cognac for their health, they pounded huge cloves of garlic in an ancient mortar, beating egg yolks with the pestle, while the fruity green olive oil dripped slowly from Celeste's fingertips and old Thérèse, with her arthritic hands, kept on beating. There was one tense moment, when the *aioli* threatened to separate.

"Slowly with the oil, Celeste! *Lentement*," protested old Thérèse.

"The oil? *Mais non!* You must *beat* faster," screeched Celeste.

About 8 o'clock, with rain drumming on the leaky roof and everyone feeling warmed by another round of cognac, we sat down to *Le Grand Aioli* – Old Thérèse, Celeste and young Thérèse, who had come fresh from Dieppe with lots of juicy news. Three grandchildren, their father and the village priest, who just happened to call and didn't seem disposed to leave once he got a whiff of the garlic. The Swedish *au pair* and me.

The mayonnaise was thick and smooth, golden yellow, aromatic. It fumed with garlic and melted onto the warm vegetables like soft butter. Celeste put the bowl in the middle of the table, with everything wreathed around it – small potatoes boiled in their skins, baby carrots and beets, raw green onions and hard-boiled eggs. We dipped each bite in the pungent *aioli* before we ate it.

The two old women fretted because there were no snails, but we had a big chunk of poached cod courtesy of the priest (though there was some discussion in the kitchen as to its age) and there were lots of rubbery little winkles.

Even without the snails, the *aioli* made a good party. A great party, with simple food, cool bottles of Provençal rosé and their rambling, gossipy stories about the writers and artists their father had entertained in the old days, when the roof didn't leak and there'd been a garlic-loving chef to make the *aioli* for them.

"Proust stayed here. He loved a good *aioli*. Picasso was here, Cocteau and Gide too – it was 1915, I think? The first war, of that I'm certain," Celeste told us, as though it were only a week ago. Beside her, Thérèse, my old garlic woman, looked happy. But then her face changed.

"And in the next war, Fenosa, the sculptor, hid in our wall behind Papa's wardrobe. They came many times, *le gestapo*, but they never found him," she said. "The Germans took our best art, our best furniture. Even Papa's dining table." She brought her hand down, smack, for emphasis, and winced in pain.

Her sister patted the knarled hand. "It doesn't matter now, *chérie*. If a table is solid, and you have something good to put on it, why must it be a work of art? *N'est-ce pas? Quoi?*"

And the wine bottle went around again.

The sisters agreed that no respectable *aioli* could be made with less than four garlic cloves per person, preferably six, but in deference to time and place I use less. At the risk of being struck dead by Provençal lightning, I also make it in a blender.

This menu is really just a French version of a fondu party, informal and fun. If you wish to add a mustard sauce or a tomato fondu, fire ahead.

TAPENADE NIÇOISE

I love the vivid flavors in this salty, slightly bitter olive paste from southern Europe. Buy good bulk olives, and add a touch more garlic if you wish.

1 1/2 cups	black olives, pitted	375 mL
3 tbsp	fresh parsley, chopped	45 mL
1	clove garlic, minced	1
1/2 tsp	pepper	2 mL
2 tbsp	anchovy paste	30 mL
2 tbsp	capers	30 mL
1 tbsp	Dijon mustard	15 mL
1 tbsp	lemon juice	15 mL
1/4 cup	olive oil	50 mL
	toasted baguette, sliced	

❖ In a blender or food processor, combine olives, parsley, garlic, pepper, anchovy paste, capers and mustard. Blend well. With machine running, drizzle in lemon juice and olive oil. Taste and adjust seasoning if necessary, but you probably won't need more salt. To serve, spread generously on slices of toasted baguette. Offer a dish of celery with it.

Makes about 2 cups (500 mL).

COOK'S NOTE: Keeps well in fridge for a week or frozen for 3 months. See Tapenade of Roasted Peppers and Sun-Dried Tomatoes (January menu) for instructions on how to toast the baguette.

Quick Grisini with Rosemary

If you have time, make these bread sticks with focaccia dough (see Red Onion Focaccia, January menu). But when time is short, here's my speedier version for fast-track cooks.

1	10 oz (311 g) tube soft bread sticks	1
1/2 cup	melted butter	125 mL
1 tsp	crushed rosemary	5 mL
1/2 cup	Parmesan cheese, freshly grated	125 mL

❖ On a flat plate, mix together rosemary and Parmesan.

Unroll bread sticks and cut each in half. Twist slightly.

Dip each stick in melted butter, then in rosemary-Parmesan mixture. Lay on an ungreased baking sheet. Bake at 375 F (190 C) about 12 minutes or until crisp and golden brown. Serve warm. Makes 16 sticks.

TEA-SMOKED EGGS

These elegantly marbled eggs are beautiful to look at, and they acquire a delicate smoky flavor from the Lapsang Souchong. Use the smallest chicken eggs you can find. Just before serving, peel half of each egg from one end and present them in a napkin-lined nest (see On the Table, April menu). They can be eaten with the mayonnaise but are excellent with nothing but salt and pepper.

16	small eggs	16
1/4 cup	loose Lapsang Souchong tea	50 mL
1/2 cup	dark soy sauce	125 mL
1 tbsp	vinegar	15 mL
1/2 tsp	allspice	2 mL
4 cups	boiling water	1 L

❖   To hard-cook the eggs, place in a saucepan, cover with cold water and bring to a boil. Turn off heat, cover and let stand 20 minutes.

Meanwhile, put tea, soy sauce, vinegar and allspice in a large saucepan. Add boiling water, cover, and let mixture steep while eggs cook.

When eggs are cool enough to handle, tap the shells gently with the back of a spoon to produce a network of tiny cracks. Put them back in the saucepan, pour the steeped liquid over them, adding a little water if necessary (they must be just covered). Turn heat to simmer. Cover and simmer 30 minutes at lowest heat. Turn off heat and leave eggs in tea mixture for 1 hour to cool. Place them, saucepan and all, in the fridge, and leave in marinade for 24 hours. Drain. They're now ready to serve.

AIOLI WITH PARSLEY

Madame would have my head for making mayo in a blender, but what she doesn't know won't hurt. You may want to increase the amount of garlic in this wonderful mayonnaise, and other herbs may be added at your personal whim. Use the best French or Italian olive oil you can find, and taste it first to be sure it's sweet.

5	cloves garlic, peeled	5
	coarse salt	
4	egg yolks	4
1 1/2 cups	olive oil	375 mL
1/4 cup	fresh parsley, chopped	50 mL

❖ Mash garlic cloves with a little coarse salt, using a mortar and pestle or the side of a knife blade, until a smooth paste forms. Place egg yolks in a blender. Blend until egg is foamy.

Add olive oil gradually in the thinnest possible stream until mixture thickens. If oil begins to separate, blend without adding more oil until it is absorbed, and then add remaining oil.

Add garlic paste and blend again, briefly. Taste for seasoning. Add parsley. Scrape mayonnaise in a bowl and cover tightly with plastic wrap. Refrigerate up to 3 days.

Makes about 2 cups (500 mL).

COOK'S NOTE: For fast-track cooks, buy a good brand of commercial mayonnaise, add garlic and parsley to taste, cover, and refrigerate 24 hours to let flavors blend.

BOILED SHRIMP

Use good-sized shrimp here, either black tiger or American white, headless but in the shell. Allow four to five shrimps per person.

1	onion, coarsely chopped	1
1	carrot, coarsely chopped	1
1	stalk celery, coarsely chopped	1
8 cups	water	2 L
1/2 cup	vinegar	125 mL
2 tbsp	pickling spice	30 mL
1 tsp	salt	5 mL
40	shrimps	40
	fresh dill or fennel fronds for garnish	

❖ Place vegetables, water, vinegar and spices in a large Dutch oven or saucepan and simmer about 15 minutes. Strain. Return stock to pot, bring to a boil and add shrimp. (If frozen, place in a colander and run under cold water until they separate easily.) As soon as shrimp turn pink, drain and run under cold water to stop the cooking. Store, covered, in fridge until ready to serve.

To serve, put shrimp on a large platter and surround with fresh dill or fennel fronds. Let everyone peel his own. Serves 8 to 10.

OVEN-BAKED SALMON

Bake the salmon far enough ahead so it's still barely warm when you're ready to serve the meal. It also can be served cold.

1	whole salmon, about 5 lbs (2.5 kg), oven-ready	1
	salt and pepper	
	celery leaves	
1	lemon, sliced	1
	butter	

❖ Preheat the oven to 450 F (230 C).

If salmon is frozen, thaw in fridge. Rinse and pat dry. Season cavity with salt and pepper. Stuff generously with celery leaves and half the lemon slices. To determine cooking time, measure fish across the back (hold the ruler perpendicular to the spine) at its widest point and allow 10 minutes baking time per inch (2.5 cm) plus 10 minutes for the foil wrap.

Lightly oil a sheet of foil large enough to wrap fish. Dot salmon with butter and lay remaining lemon slices on it. Place salmon on a baking sheet on the center rack. After about 20 minutes, open the foil and check for doneness. (Flesh should be opaque.)

When salmon is done to taste, cool in the foil. Unwrap, remove skin (it will peel off in pieces with a little help from a small, sharp knife) and place salmon on a serving platter. Garnish with celery leaves and lemon slices or lay on a bed of dill fronds. Serves 8 to 10.

reach and set wine bottles on the table so people can help themselves. The colors and shapes in the food are so gorgeous you hardly need other decoration, but tulips are in season, and a glass or pottery jug of white tulips and pussy willows, or a mixed bunch of reds and yellows with a few irises tucked in, is the essence of spring.

CUCUMBER-DILL SAUCE WITH MUSTARD AND TARRAGON

This luxurious fresh cream sauce is especially good with salmon and also complements the shellfish.

If you're desperate about calories, substitute skim milk yogurt for the whipping cream.

1 cup	cream, whipped	250 mL
3 tbsp	tarragon vinegar	45 mL
1/2 cup	cucumber, finely chopped	125 mL
2 tbsp	fresh dill, chopped	30 mL
1 tsp	mustard seed	5 mL
1/2 tsp	tarragon leaves	2 mL
	salt and pepper	

❖ Beat vinegar into whipped cream. Press cucumber in a sieve to remove excess juice. Add to vinegar and whipped cream with seasonings and serve in a bowl. Makes about 2 cups (500 mL).

In the Bottle

No shy flavors here, so this is no place for timid wines. For a sharp palate cleanser after the tapenade, an acidic wine like Muscadet de Sevre et Maine should do the trick. A rosé from Provence also stands up to the garlic. With main dishes, try a fat sauvignon blanc, one with lots of fruit but enough herbal edge to...

SPRING VEGETABLE BASKET

Almost any vegetable will go well here, including broccoli, fennel, green beans, tiny artichokes, steamed green onions or radishes. Just buy the best quality you can find. In France, you can buy baked baby beets in the markets. Here, canned rosebud beets will serve as a handy alternative.

24	stalks asparagus	24
16	young carrots with tops	16
16	small new red potatoes	16
16	baby beets	16

❖ Wash asparagus and break off the tough end of each stalk. Trim stalks if necessary. Scrub but do not peel carrots and potatoes. If potatoes are no larger than eggs, leave whole, otherwise cut in half. Leave about 1/2 inch (2 cm) of green stem on each carrot.

Steam each vegetable until tender-crisp. If you aren't going to serve immediately, stop the cooking by drenching vegetables in cold water. Cover and refrigerate. Reheat before serving – these vegetables can be served at room temperature or warm but should be neither screamin' hot nor ice cold.

To serve, arrange the vegetables on a pretty platter, bunching each type together in an attractive way. Serves 8 to 10.

COOK'S NOTE: Because of the sauces (or dips), most people will think of this as a forkless fondue. You might like to add a basket of raw vegetables as well – sliced zucchini, green onions, radishes, pepper strips, cherry tomatoes, whatever looks good in the market.

...bring out vegetable flavors. A good choice with the salmon and aioli is Mondavi's Chevrignon, a rich and aromatic wine that isn't overwhelmed by garlic. A well-chilled Gamay de Touraine also works – it's like a Beaujolais but fresher and simpler, with an utterly delicious taste of ripe fruit.

DOUBLE CHOCOLATE CARROT CAKE WITH BROWN SUGAR ICING

This is a terrific cake to begin with, but the aroma of freshly crushed cloves gives it an extra edge. It's easy to crush whole cloves with a rolling pin or a pestle and mortar.

1 cup	butter	250 mL
1 1/2 cups	sugar	375 mL
3	eggs	3
1 tsp	baking powder	5 mL
1/2 tsp	nutmeg	2 mL
2 tbsp	baking cocoa	30 mL
2 1/2 cups	flour	625 mL
1 tsp	cinnamon	5 mL
4	whole cloves, finely crushed	4
1 tbsp	vanilla	15 mL
1/2 cup	water	125 mL
2 cups	carrots, shredded	500 mL
3/4 cup	nuts, chopped	175 mL
1 cup	white chocolate chips	250 mL

❖ Preheat oven to 350 F (180 C).

Cream butter and sugar until light and fluffy. Add eggs one at a time, beating well after each addition. Sift together dry ingredients and add to creamed mixture alternately with vanilla and water. Fold in carrots, nuts and chips. Turn into prepared 9 x 13 inch (4 L) pan. Bake 45 minutes or until cake tests done. Cool and frost. Serves 10 to 12.

BROWN SUGAR ICING

This is like the best brown sugar fudge you've ever made. A cake with this should be illegal.

1/4 cup	butter	50 mL
1 cup	brown sugar, packed	250 mL
1/3 cup	cream	75 mL
1 tsp	vanilla	5 mL
3/4 cup	icing sugar, sifted	75 mL

❖ Put butter, brown sugar and cream in a medium pan and bring to a boil. Cook 2 minutes. Remove from heat, add vanilla, sift in icing sugar and beat with an electric mixer until smooth and creamy. Spread while still warm.

Fish Story

There's something about fish that intimidates me. They're such a secretive lot, swimming endlessly in the cool dark, patrolling hidden places.

But there are some fish that I understand because they have so often been on my plate and occasionally on my hook.

One childhood summer my parents built a cottage on a deep, cold lake in central Saskatchewan. They were avid fishermen, so Friday nights we'd drive to the little pink house beside the lake, and I'd watch them putter away across the water, trolling back and forth with a red leader or a silver spoon or whatever the local grapevine predicted would lure a fish that night. They'd stay on the lake until dark, by which time I would have concocted something of a one-dish nature in the oven of the wood stove. If they'd been lucky, whatever was in the oven would be canceled forthwith because we had real fish to fry.

Shortly after sunrise they'd be off again, trolling around the likelier spots, waiting for a bite. On that lake, the favorite catch happened to be the big, meaty jackfish that some people called northern pike. A jack is a fighting game fish, and the ones in our lake usually weighed about eight pounds but could go as high as forty, or so rumor had it, though we never caught anything that big.

I liked the way the jacks looked, so sleek and bluey-green, with their fierce teeth and pointed jaws. So did Mom, and when somebody wrote a cookbook explaining how

*Thai Shrimp Soup with
Lemon Grass*

*Bulgur Wheat Salad with
Bacon and Avocado*

*Sweet Corn Bannock with
Jalapenos and Cheese*

Mom's Freshwater Fish Fry

Lemon Tarragon Vinaigrette

Shoestring Hot-Hots

*Strawberry Gelato with Fresh
Strawberry Sauce*

the flavor of jackfish was insipid and needed a little perking up, she was indignant. It was true that *some* people scorned it because in the wrong water a jackfish could be slimy and flabby, but those were high water years, and when we sank our teeth into the firm, milk-white flesh crisply fried and only an hour out of the water, we sat at a privileged table.

I always knew when the fishermen were back because my dog would go into a frenzy of barking and tail wagging. Then we'd all go out in the backyard where Dad's fileting table stood, and Mom would sit on her hammock with a cup of coffee, swinging gently, watching while the wind ruffled Dad's hair and the knife flashed in the lowering sun. The poplars rustled, the lake made lapping noises just over the hill, and I knew that a great fish feed was only an hour away.

Among the family cooks there were rules about fish. Grandma established them years before, while cooking vast fish breakfasts for my grandfather, his eight children and the assortment of visiting clergy, hired men and hangers-on that sat around her table.

Mom kept the faith, so her fish had to be fried in solid shortening, in a pan so hot it smoked. Oil wasn't even considered, nor was batter, which she looked upon as an unnecessary frippery. Her method was to dip the piece of fish in seasoned flour and lay it gently in the bubbling fat, and when it was *really* golden, she'd turn it over with one deft motion and fry the other side. She finished it in the oven, where it became delicately crisp and the flesh grew meltingly tender.

When we ate fish, that's all we ate, with lemon or vinegar, unless we had company who didn't know about Mom's fish and looked like they expected something else on their plates. In that event, she'd eke out the meal with fried potatoes and sliced tomatoes, but when we ate according to our own whim, we just ate fish.

Except for the shrimp soup, which takes a bit of shopping for the ingredients, this is one of the simplest meals in the book. The soup is from Bangkok, the fish is pure Saskatchewan, the potatoes were inspired by a friend from Jaipur, India, and the wheat salad makes a perfect foil for the rest of the meal.

THAI SHRIMP SOUP WITH LEMON GRASS

Do make a trip to an Asian market for the lemon grass, kaffir lime leaves, fish sauce and chili paste, and do use shrimps in the shell because the flavor of this soup is pure magic if you do it right. Be careful when handling the tiny green chilies (called *nam prik* in the Asian markets), as their oils are lethally hot.

1 lb	uncooked shrimp in shells	500 g
2	sticks fresh lemon grass	2
4	dried kaffir lime leaves or 1 tbsp (15 mL) finely grated lime rind	4
6 cups	chicken stock	1 1/2 L
1 tbsp	fish sauce (or salt to taste)	15 mL
3 tbsp	fresh lime juice	45 mL
1 tsp	chili paste	5 mL
3	fresh hot green chilies, finely sliced	3
3 tbsp	fresh coriander leaves	45 mL

❖ Wash and peel shrimp, reserving shells. Cover and refrigerate.

Starting from the bottom end, slice lemon grass diagonally until you're into the leafy part. Throw the leafy part away and crush slices just to bruise them.

Put lemon grass, kaffir lime, chicken stock and shrimp shells in a large soup pot. Bring to a boil. Lower heat and simmer 20 minutes. Strain stock and return to the pot. Add fish sauce, lime juice and chili paste. Mix and taste again, adding more fish sauce or lime juice to taste. Store in fridge until serving time.

To serve, reheat the stock and add peeled shrimp, sliced if they're too large. As soon as the flesh turns opaque and pink, serve the soup, garnished with green chilies and whole coriander leaves. Serves 8 to 10.

NOTE: Do not rub your eyes or touch your lips while working with chilies.

BULGUR WHEAT SALAD WITH BACON AND AVOCADO

I love the textures here, with slightly chewy wheat, crisp bacon, creamy soft avocado. It's a terrific salad all by itself or with rye bread, and it goes especially well with this meal. If you don't like bulgur wheat, substitute cooked brown rice. Tabouleh (wheat salad) mix also can be used to speed things up a bit.

To steep bulgur wheat, pour boiling water over it, using half as much water as wheat. Cover and let the cracked grains steep (absorb the hot water) about 45 minutes, then drain. This will plump the cracked grains just enough so they will easily absorb the dressing.

3 cups	steeped bulgur wheat	750 mL
1	avocado, diced	1
3	strips bacon, diced and fried	3
12 to 14	cherry tomatoes, halved	12 to 14
1/2 cup	ripe olives, sliced	125 mL
4	green onions, sliced	4
3	garlic cloves, mashed	3
1 tsp	salt	5 mL
1/4 cup	red wine vinegar	50 mL
	juice and finely grated rind of 1 lime	
1/3 cup	olive oil	75 mL
1/2 tsp	black pepper	2 mL
	iceberg lettuce, shredded	
	cherry tomatoes and black olives for garnish	

❖ Mash garlic in salt. Place in a blender with vinegar, lime juice and rind, olive oil and black pepper. Toss with steeped bulgur wheat, avocado, bacon, cherry tomatoes, olives and green onions.

Let salad stand, refrigerated, at least 1 hour (and up to 6 hours) before serving.

To serve, line a platter with shredded iceberg lettuce. Mound the salad in the middle. Garnish with extra cherry tomatoes and black olives. Serves 8 to 10.

SWEET CORN BANNOCK WITH JALAPENOS AND CHEESE

My Dad used to make frying pan bannock, a native Indian bread that we loved with butter and strawberry jam. My Southwestern version is speedier and has a few frills, including the canned jalapenoes.

2 1/2 cups	biscuit mix	625 mL
1/2 tsp	salt	2 mL
1/2 tsp	dry mustard	2 mL
1/2 cup	Cheddar cheese, grated	250 mL
1/2 cup	canned jalapenoes, diced	125 mL
1	10 oz (284 mL) can creamed corn	1
1	egg, beaten	1
	soft butter	

❖ Preheat oven to 425 F (220 C).

In a medium bowl, combine biscuit mix, salt and dry mustard. With a fork, stir in cheese, peppers, creamed corn and egg until a soft dough forms. (Dough should be soft but manageable. If it's too dry, add a little milk.) Turn onto a floured surface. Knead gently 10 to 12 times, until no longer sticky. Form dough into a small round loaf and slash a cross in the top. Place on a greased baking sheet. Slather with soft butter.

Bake 12 to 15 minutes or until golden brown. Remove from oven and repeat soft butter treatment. Return to oven about 5 minutes or until done. Let cool 10 minutes before slicing. Serve on a large board with a sharp knife or tucked into a napkin-lined basket. Serves 8 to 10.

On the Table

Once at a garage sale I bought an oversized clam shell. For this dinner, I fill it with lemons, tuck three or four small sea shells among them and add sprigs of cedar, which look oddly like seaweed. The soup is served in a collection of bowl-sized shells and napkins go in shell napkin rings. If you don't have shells, use clear glass bowls.

In the Bottle

With such dramatic flavors in stunning juxtaposition, the food will dominate the wine no matter what. So go for utilitarian wine that cleanses the palate of the last flavor and prepares it for the next. A simple chilled German trocken is a good choice. Tart and bone-dry, it washes...

MOM'S FRESHWATER FISH FRY

The terrible pollution of our freshwater lakes and rivers has already contaminated much of our fish. If you're lucky enough to have access to a clean lake or river, count your blessings.

Big, freshly caught jackfish, lake whitefish, pickerel or northern pike work well here. If you can't find good freshwater fish, halibut or cod can be substituted. The quality of the fish is the most important thing.

Great fried fish is a luxury, but it does tend to make your house smell like a chip shop, so turn on the fan before you begin.

4 lbs	fish filets	2 kg
1 cup	milk	250 mL
1 cup	flour seasoned with salt and pepper	250 mL
	vegetable oil for frying	
	celery leaves for garnish	

❖ Preheat oven to 325 F (160 C).

In a large cast iron frying pan, heat 2 inches (6 cm) of bland vegetable oil until it begins to wiggle slightly. Dip filets in milk, then in seasoned flour. Slip filets in hot oil, two or three at a time. When nicely golden, turn each carefully, using a pancake turner or reliable tongs. Fry flip side until similarly golden. Drain on paper.

When all fish is fried, place on a wire rack arranged over a baking sheet to catch stray drips. Bake about 15 minutes or until fish barely begins to flake with a fork. Arrange on a large platter garnished with celery leaves. Serve hot, with Lemon Tarragon Vinaigrette. Serve 8 to 10.

LEMON TARRAGON VINAIGRETTE

Serve this in a small pitcher on a plate with lots of lemon wedges, so guests can drizzle a little over their fish and then add as much lemon juice as they wish. If you don't have tarragon vinegar, add 1/2 tsp (2 mL) dried tarragon to the sauce.

3/4 cup	lemon juice	175 mL
1/4 cup	tarragon vinegar	50 mL
1/4 cup	water	50 mL
2 tbsp	salad oil	30 mL
1 tsp	dry mustard	5 mL
1 tsp	sugar	5 mL
1/2 tsp	salt	2 mL
5	drops of Tabasco sauce	5
2 tbsp	fresh parsley, minced	30 mL

❖ Whisk all ingredients together in a small bowl. When sugar has dissolved, pour in a small saucepan and bring to a boil. Immediately remove from heat and serve.

Makes about 1 1/2 cups (375 mL).

…away the last lingering spice. Rosé is a choice again, particularly with Thai shrimp soup. A burly yet fragrant wine like a Dao white from Portugal stands up to vinaigrette and does something for fish. A neutral white like pinot blanc does nicely too, and it finds a gentle harmony with corn bannock.

SHOESTRING HOT-HOTS

Stir-frying frozen shoestring potatoes with warm, highly aromatic spices gives them a whole new personality. Wonderful with fish.

1	garlic clove	1
1 tsp	ground cumin	5 mL
2 tsp	curry powder	10 mL
1 tsp	mustard seed	5 mL
1 tsp	ginger	5 mL
1	dried chili pepper, crushed	1
1 tsp	salt	5 mL
2 lbs	frozen shoestring potatoes	1 kg
1 tbsp	oil	15 mL
2 tsp	white vinegar	10 mL

❖ Crush garlic, spices, chili pepper and salt with the back of a knife.

Cook frozen shoestring potatoes according to package directions. (Do not over cook.)

In a large wok or frying pan, fry crushed spice mixture in oil until browned, dry and aromatic.

Add potatoes and sprinkle with vinegar. Stir-fry potatoes until they've been acquainted with the spices, about 2 minutes. Pile them onto a platter and serve at once. Serves 8 to 10.

STRAWBERRY GELATO WITH
FRESH STRAWBERRY SAUCE

Once, in the old Umbrian town of Perugia, I went on an ice cream binge and sampled half a dozen flavors of the freshest, most delicious *gelati* I'd ever found. The best was the strawberry cream, and this is as close as I can come to the real thing.

The trick is to serve it while it's still lusciously fresh, before hard ice crystals form.

4 cups	ripe strawberries	1 L
1 1/2 cups	sugar	375 mL
1/4 cup	liquid honey	50 mL
1/2 cup	water	125 mL
2	egg whites	2
1 cup	whipping cream	250 mL

❖ Place berries in the food processor and purée.

In a medium saucepan, combine sugar, honey and water. Stir over medium heat until sugar dissolves. Cook sugar mixture to 234 F (112 C) on a candy thermometer or until syrup hairs from a spoon.

In a medium bowl, beat egg whites until they form stiff peaks but are not dry. Continuing to beat, drizzle hot syrup into egg whites. Beat until cool and thick. Stir in berry purée.

In a medium bowl, whip cream until soft peaks form. Fold into berry mixture. Pour in an ice cream freezer container and freeze according to manufacturer's directions. Serve within a few hours. Serves 8 to 10.

Fresh Strawberry Sauce

2 cups	ripe strawberries	500 mL
1 tsp	orange rind, grated	5 mL
juice of 1 orange		
1/4 cup	liquid honey	50 mL

❖ Wash berries and pour honey over them. Add orange rind and juice. Place everything in a blender or food processor and reduce to a coarse purée. Serve as soon as possible with Fresh Strawberry Gelato. Makes about 1 1/2 cups (375 mL).

Happy Birthday Anyway

A few words now about that ever-popular celebration for all seasons, the birthday party.

When a woman is young, approaching, say, her sixth birthday, somebody is certain to plan a party. It's a rite of passage.

It's also the day on which she learns one of life's little truths: birthday parties are not all they're cracked up to be.

Right off the bat, there's the question of party clothes. They're uncomfortable. They're made that way on purpose so we civilized humans don't get carried away with our own importance during these benchmark celebrations. Party clothes are itchy, stiff and too tight in all the wrong places. Ask any man who has ever struggled into a tux. It's the way of the world, from christenings through graduations, bar mitzvahs through funerals. For all I know, shrouds are itchy.

And so, to party time. A lot of little kids arrive, two of whom she likes. She wishes everybody else were in Timbuktu. Her mother did the guest list.

Now for the gifts. She's dutifully ecstatic about the toy iron and tries to be grateful for a doll that cries, wets its diaper and spits up. (Oh joy.) She wanted a chemistry set, but never mind – she can play baby-sitter until she's tired of the stupid doll. Then she can play laundry woman.

SIX

JUNE

Ming's Birthday Slush

Seafood Fritters with
Hot Sweet Rhubarb Chutney

Mushroom Plate Bread

Cucumber Salsa

Beefsteak Tomatoes with
Fresh Basil

Barbecue Roots

Pork, Chicken and
Beef Satays

Peanut Dipping Sauce

Maple Angel Cake with
Maple Mousse

Warm Plum Cobbler with
Raspberries

Games next. She has to share, take turns and let many tiny, imperfect strangers muck about with her gifts. Her patience is wearing thin. During musical chairs (a game she hates, but nobody asked her), there's a fight over a technicality, and when she punches the instigator right on the nose, he runs sniveling to her mother. The birthday girl gets to spend the rest of her party in her room, while everybody else including the tattling little sniveler devours her birthday cake. Her misery is complete.

Many birthdays pass. One night, just as Father Time is snipping yet another year off her allotted span, she's in a restaurant, having a quiet celebration with friends.

Suddenly, a spotlight is aimed at her head. Her friends grin inanely. Half the room turns to stare.

Now seven waiters gather around her table, led by one near-sighted youth banging on a frying pan, inches from her left ear.

They bellow Happy Birthday, Dear Mmphmph, because they don't know her name, and they don't care. Somebody plops a funny hat on her head. Somebody else gives her a noisemaker.

She wants to leave, but it's not over yet. The choir roars into the second verse, something about "May you live a thousand years, drink a thousand beers, get pl–astered you ba–ad girl" and so forth. She smiles and decides that strangling would be too kind for the cretinous youth banging on the pan.

And now the whole room is staring.

Where's the nearest exit?

But no. She can't leave yet, there's cake. A big one, swathed in fluorescent pink icing, a mountain of edible oil product, certain to be hideously fattening, and heaven knows what it does to arteries.

Forty-odd candles are not a lot, as birthdays go, but before the ceremonial first cut can be made, several have dripped themselves into oblivion. They sputter in the sea of icing, and they die. Fine, she thinks, just what I wanted, a bunch of dead candles on my cake. It's prophetic.

She decides to spend her next 40 birthdays in seclusion.

Birthday girls deserve the best, and this barbecue is just that. I love the exciting combinations of herbs and spices and the smoky grilled meats against the soft, round flavors and textures of the potatoes and the homey dessert.

MING'S BIRTHDAY SLUSH

I had this pleasantly fruity, mildly alcoholic punch at a birthday party in Vancouver, but Ming swears she got it from her sister in Hong Kong. Either way, it goes well with the spicy appetizer fritters if you aren't into wine.

10 cups	boiling water, divided	2.5 L
2 cups	sugar	500 mL
4	tea bags	4
1	12 oz (375 mL) can frozen lemonade, undiluted	1
1	12 oz (375 mL) can frozen orange juice, undiluted	1
2 cups	Rose's lime cordial	500 mL
2 cups	vodka	500 mL
2 quarts	tonic water	2 L
	lime twists and mint leaves for garnish	

❖ Dissolve sugar in 8 cups (2 L) of boiling water. Reserve.

Pour remaining 2 cups (500 mL) boiling water over tea bags, cover and steep until tea is very strong. In a large plastic ice cream pail, mix together sugar water, tea, lemonade, orange juice, lime cordial and vodka. Cover and freeze at least 4 hours.

At serving time, fill desired glass 1/2 to 3/4 full of slush mixture, top with tonic water and garnish with lime twists and mint leaves. Serve with a straw. Makes about 1.5 gallons (6 L).

SEAFOOD FRITTERS WITH HOT SWEET RHUBARB CHUTNEY

Use small cooked shrimp or broken shrimp, sometimes marketed as salad shrimp. The recipe calls for only 1/2 cup (125 mL) of beer, so the cook will have to drink the rest. Ah, shucks.

2 cups	cooked shrimp, diced	500 mL
4	large eggs	4
1 cup	flour	250 mL
1/2 cup	beer	125 mL
1 1/2 tsp	baking powder	7 mL
2 tsp	curry powder	10 mL
1 tsp	ginger, freshly grated	5 mL
1 tsp	salt	5 mL
1/4 cup	sweet red pepper, finely diced	50 mL
1/2 cup	tiny green peas, fresh or frozen	125 mL
1	small onion, finely diced	1
	vegetable oil for frying	

❖ If using large shrimp, chop to the size of tiny peas.

In a medium bowl, beat together eggs, flour, beer, baking powder, curry powder, ginger and salt. Fold in shrimp meat, red pepper, peas and onion.

In a deep frying pan or deep-fryer, heat 2 inches (6 cm) of oil to 375 F (190 C). Drop mixture by tablespoons in the oil and fry until golden brown on both sides. Drain well on paper towels before serving hot.

Makes about 36 oddly shaped fritters. Serves 8 to 10.

COOK'S NOTE: For fast-track cooks, make these some night when you haven't another thing in the world to do. Cool and lay out on wax paper-lined baking sheets. Cover with aluminum foil and freeze. To serve, reheat, uncovered, in a 375 F (190 C) oven until hot through and crisp.

HOT SWEET RHUBARB CHUTNEY

This is so good with seafood fritters that you'll be grateful for leftovers because it's just as good with cold meats or grilled chicken.

4	medium onions, finely chopped	4
4 cups	rhubarb, diced	1 L
1 cup	golden raisins	250 mL
1 1/2	vinegar	375 mL
3 cups	brown sugar	750 mL
1 tsp	salt	5 mL
1 tsp	black pepper	5 mL
1 tsp	whole mustard	5 mL
1 tsp	curry powder	5 mL
1 tsp	ground allspice	5 mL
2 tsp	cinnamon	10 mL
2 tbsp	ginger, freshly minced	30 mL
3	cloves garlic, minced	3

❖ Put all ingredients in a large, heavy Dutch oven. Bring to a boil and immediately reduce heat to simmer. Continue to simmer until thickened, stirring often. Pour in a large jar and refrigerate until needed. This keeps well in the fridge for several weeks. Makes about 6 cups (1.5 L).

MUSHROOM PLATE BREAD

Fast and delicious, this is a versatile side dish to make whenever you need something to round out a salad meal or to accompany meats.

1/2 cup	red onion, diced	125 mL
1 cup	white mushrooms, sliced	250 mL
1 tbsp	butter	15 mL
1 cup	milk	250 mL
2	eggs	2
1 cup	biscuit mix	250 mL
3/4 cup	mozzarella cheese, grated	175 mL
1 tsp	salt	5 mL
1/4 cup	Parmesan cheese, grated	50 mL

❖ Preheat oven to 400 F (200 C). Butter a 9 inch (1 L) pie plate.

In a small frying pan, sauté onion and mushrooms in butter.

Lightly beat together milk, eggs and biscuit mix. Stir in mozzarella, salt and fried vegetables. Pour mixture into buttered pie plate and sprinkle with Parmesan.

Bake about 30 minutes or until golden brown. Cool 10 minutes before slicing into wedges. Serves 8.

COOK'S NOTE: For variation, this bread can be made with sweet peppers, tomatoes, green onions, in fact almost any vegetable, diced and fried. It is also excellent made with blue cheese, onions and walnuts instead of vegetables and mozzarella. The bread freezes well too. For a crowd, double the recipe and use 2 pie plates.

CUCUMBER SALSA

Cool, sharp and sweet, this traditional Thai condiment is a delicious accompaniment to barbecued satays. Buy slender cucumbers, and take extra care when handling the tiny, hot chilies. If you can't find fresh ones, use one dried red chile, crumbled.

1 cup	rice vinegar	250 mL
1/2 cup	oil	125 mL
1/2 cup	sugar	125 mL
1 tsp	salt	5 mL
2	fresh red chilies, minced	2
8	shallots, sliced	8
2	English cucumbers, quartered, thinly sliced	2
1/4 cup	fresh coriander, chopped	50 mL

❖ In a medium bowl, mix together vinegar, oil, sugar and salt. Stir in chilies, shallots, cucumber and coriander. Set aside to marinate for at least 1 hour. Makes about 4 cups (1 L).

BEEFSTEAK TOMATOES WITH FRESH BASIL

Nothing complicated about this, yet it's a perfect accompaniment
to grilled meat of any kind. If you can't find beefsteak tomatoes, use
twice as many Roma tomatoes. Either way, be sure the tomatoes are
dead ripe and on the warm side to bring out the best flavor.

4	ripe beefsteak tomatoes	4
1 tsp	sugar	5 mL
2 tbsp	red wine vinegar	30 mL
2 tbsp	olive oil	30 mL
	large bunch fresh basil for garnish	

❖   Bring tomatoes to room temperature. Better still, let them
stand 20 minutes in the sun.

About 15 minutes ahead of time, slice and arrange tomatoes on a
platter. Sprinkle sparsely with sugar. Drizzle with vinegar and oil.

Chop about 1/2 cup (125 mL) of basil leaves and sprinkle over
tomatoes. Remove other leaves from stem and tuck them here and
there among tomato slices. Cover the platter and leave it at room
temperature (no longer than 15 minutes) until serving. Serves 10.

BARBECUE ROOTS

Root vegetables are always solid, comforting fare. These are like scalloped potatoes, only better. Perfect with the spicy meats in this meal, they were inspired by a recipe from CBC radio personality Peter Gzowski.

6	large baking potatoes, scrubbed	6
1	large carrot	1
2	large Spanish onions	2
2	garlic cloves	2
	salt and pepper	
	fresh parsley, chopped	
1 cup	light cottage cheese	250 mL
1/2 cup	Cheddar cheese, shredded	125 mL

❖ Cut potatoes into 1/2 inch (1 cm) slices. Slice carrot and onions thinly. On a large square of buttered, heavy-duty foil, place half the potato slices in a single layer. Top with half the sliced carrot and onion. Sprinkle with salt, pepper and chopped parsley.

Purée cottage cheese and garlic in a blender or food processor and pour over the vegetables. Sprinkle with Cheddar. Layer with remaining vegetables. Now fold foil over, sealing tightly.

Grill over medium-hot coals about 20 minutes. Turn carefully, and grill 15 to 20 minutes longer or until vegetables are tender.Carrots take longer than you expect, so give the whole package an extra few minutes if necessary. Serves 10.

In the Bottle

The seafood fritter will take any white, but the sweet rhubarb chutney might overwhelm. Try a classic apéritif, kir royale. Put a teaspoon of black currant or raspberry liqueur in each chilled champagne flute and fill with cold sparkling wine – Spanish cava, German sekt or dry Italian. The color is lovely, the taste is appealing. It's a bit sweet but goes well with…

PORK, CHICKEN AND BEEF SATAYS

In Bangkok, as night falls on Silom Road, the smell of these skewers of spicy meat grilling on little charcoal stoves is a potent incense. They're the definitive street food and terrific at a party.

PORK AND CHICKEN

1 lb	skinless, boneless chicken breast	500 g
1 lb	boneless pork loin	500 g
1/2 tsp	turmeric	2 mL
1 tsp	curry powder	5 mL
1 tsp	salt	5 mL
1/2 cup	unsweetened coconut milk	125 mL
1/4 cup	oil	50 mL

BEEF

1 lb	beef, top round	500 g
1/2 tsp	whole coriander seeds	2 mL
1/2 cup	vegetable oil	125 mL
1/2 cup	soy sauce	125 mL
	cilantro leaves for garnish	

❖ Cut pork and chicken into strips, 3 inches (7 cm) long by roughly 1/2 inch (1/2 cm) wide. Place chicken and pork in a large shallow dish. Sprinkle evenly with turmeric, curry powder and salt. Pour coconut milk and oil over meat and mix to coat thoroughly. Cover and refrigerate at least 1 hour.

Now cut beef into strips the same size as the pork and chicken. In a small dry frying pan, toast coriander seeds over high heat until fragrant and golden brown, about 30 seconds. In a mortar, crush seeds finely. In a small bowl, turn beef in mixture of oil and soy sauce. Sprinkle beef with crushed coriander seeds. Cover and refrigerate at least 1 hour.

Soak 48, 8 inch (20 cm) bamboo skewers in a bowl of water for at least 20 minutes.

Preheat the barbecue and oil the grill.

Thread pork, chicken and beef onto separate skewers without crowding. Arrange the skewers on the grill, and cook 5 inches (12 cm) from the heat, turning a few times, about 4 minutes or until meat is browned and cooked to taste. Arrange skewers of meat on a large platter, garnished with a bunch of cilantro leaves. Serve hot on skewers with Cucumber Salsa and Peanut Dipping Sauce on the side.

Serves 10 to 12.

PEANUT DIPPING SAUCE

Tamarind and fish sauce are both available, in tiny containers, at Indian or Asian markets.

1/2 cup	unsweetened coconut milk	125 mL
1 cup	chunky peanut butter	250 mL
1/2 tsp	Tabasco sauce (or to taste)	2 mL
1 tbsp	brown sugar	15 mL
2 tsp	fish sauce	10 mL
1/2 tsp	instant tamarind	2 mL
2 tsp	hot water	10 mL

❖ In a medium saucepan, bring coconut milk to a boil over high heat. Reduce heat to moderate and stir in peanut butter, Tabasco, brown sugar and fish sauce. Stir tamarind in hot water and add to sauce. Bring just to a simmer, stirring constantly. Remove from heat and let cool to room temperature. Refrigerate in a covered jar up to 2 weeks.

Makes about 1 1/2 cups (375 mL). Recipe may be doubled.

...seafood. The satays with peanut sauce are assertive, and you may wish to continue with the kir. Otherwise, think of a sweetish fumé blanc to go with the light meats and pick up the sweetness of puréed peanuts. Cooled zinfandel has the character to stand up to the peanuts and pairs the meat nicely. A German auslese of recent vintage is a good match for the cake.

MAPLE ANGEL BIRTHDAY CAKE WITH MAPLE MOUSSE

On special birthdays, my mother made angel food cakes from scratch, using 13 egg whites per cake. I find that an angel food cake mix works just as well and doesn't leave me wondering what to do with 13 egg yolks.

1	white angel food mix	1
2 tsp	maple flavoring	10 mL
1/2 cup	walnuts, ground or finely chopped	125 mL

❖ Make angel food cake according to package directions, adding maple flavoring with the water. After beating, fold in walnuts using 8 quick folds, turning the bowl 1/4 turn with each fold.

Pour batter in ungreased angel food pan and bake according to package directions. Cool thoroughly in the pan before removing. May be made days ahead and frozen.

Just before serving, dust cake with icing sugar by sprinkling no more than 1 tbsp (15 mL) through a sieve. Serve with Maple Mousse on the side. Serves 10.

MAPLE MOUSSE

Some cooks make a zabaglione version of this, using only the yolks. I prefer a prairie-style seafoam made with whole eggs. If you're using a high grade of maple syrup, you may want to bump up the flavor a tad with 1 tsp (5 mL) of maple flavoring.

2	eggs	2
1/2 cup	maple syrup	125 mL ·
	pinch of salt and cream of tartar	
1 cup	whipping cream	250 mL

❖ In the top of a double boiler, over barely simmering water, beat together eggs and maple syrup with an electric mixer. When they begin to foam, add salt and cream of tartar. Continue beating until mixture begins to form peaks, roughly 7 minutes. Remove from heat and continue beating until it acquires a gloss. Stir in maple flavoring if desired. Cool.

Whip cream until stiff and fold into maple mixture. Taste for sweetness. Pour in a serving dish, cover tightly and chill. Makes about 3 cups (750 mL).

WARM PLUM COBBLER WITH RASPBERRIES

Why two desserts or even three? Because birthday girls deserve to be spoiled.

Some cobblermakers put the crust on the bottom, others put it on top. Either way, the crust must never be too precise. Rather, it should look a bit tattered and casual and rosy, like the birthday girl herself.

3 cups	blue plums, quartered	750 mL
2 cups	ripe raspberries	500 mL
1 cup	sugar	250 mL
2 tbsp	quick-cooking tapioca	30 mL
1/2 tsp	almond extract	2 mL
1 1/2 cups	all-purpose flour	375 mL
2 tbsp	sugar	30 mL
1 tbsp	baking powder	15 mL
1/2 tsp	salt	2 mL
3 tbsp	butter	45 mL
1/2 cup	ground almonds	125 mL
2/3 cup	milk	150 mL

❖ Preheat oven to 400 F (200 C).

Place plums in a buttered 11 x 7 inch (2 L) baking dish. Mix together 1 cup (250 mL) sugar, tapioca and almond extract. Toss with plums. Gently toss sweetened plums with raspberries.

Sift together flour, 2 tbsp (30 mL) sugar, baking powder and salt. Cut in butter until mixture resembles fine crumbs. With a fork, stir in ground almonds. Add milk and mix lightly with a fork to make a soft dough. (It may be necessary to add a little more milk.)

Turn dough onto a floured board and knead 10 to 12 times. Roll dough into a rough rectangle slightly smaller than baking dish and lay it over the mixed fruit. If you wish to gild the lily, lightly dust the dough with sugar and cinnamon. Poke about 6 holes in the dough.

Bake about 30 minutes or until topping is golden and fruit bubbles through the top. Serve warm. Serves 8 to 10.

COOK'S NOTE: If nectarines are on sale and looking good, substitute them for the plums. They're a delicious combination.

Birds, Berries and Summer Weddings...

Saskatchewan in high summer. Another family wedding, this one on the brink of berry season.

First things first, and on a white-hot wedding morning, Grandpa is in his garden, worrying over his raspberries. The canes look healthy, but the leaves are turning yellow. The local ag-rep, called in to consult, offered too much choice for comfort – it's either spider mites or low iron. Maybe both. Or maybe something else. So how's a man supposed to know what to do? Douse 'em or dose 'em? Soap suds or iron filings?

Then there's the crisis in the strawberry patch, currently under siege by many pesky robins. Between gophers and birds, there's no peace for a man and his garden. He's declared war on all birds, "and that includes those darned robins, they should be eating worms anyway," but this morning when I visited the patch he was having little success.

Under the hot prairie sun, berries reddening against the earth are an easy target for any passing bird that isn't blind or stupid. As Grandpa's first line of defence, he plants tall plastic sunflowers with windmill petals. The combination of movement and noise is designed to discourage berry thievery. In the feeble breeze, his windmills whir dutifully and whiz fitfully, but these birds are a sassy bunch, and they attack the berries with unbirdlike concentration.

*Ricotta al Forno with
Baby Radishes*

Grilled Chicken Indienne

Garden Frittatas

*Thai Rice Salad with
Lime Vinaigrette*

Rhubarb Berry Custard Pie

*Peanut Butter
Wedding Cookies with
White Chocolate Glaze*

Iced Tea with Mint and Lime

Orange Rhubarb Spritzers

Well, he's not finished. Not by a long shot. If there's nothing left for the invaders to eat, they'll either starve or retreat. It's a modified version of the scorched earth policy. With a large bowl and a determined right hand, he picks the entire crop. Every berry, whether ripe, green or middling, is delivered to the kitchen.

Grandma ponders the green berries, but before she can deliver an opinion, Aunt Bea runs in with more bad news from the berry front. It's a letter from Great Aunt Ella, who writes from Elmira, Ontario, that she's just paid $1.99 for a miniscule box of strawberries, in fact thirteen. "I counted," says Ella.

Around the table, the assembled aunts mutter over the teacups. Thirteen berries, imagine. They do some rapid math and are aghast at the price per berry. It's robbery. Ella was taken.

Big discussion. Gouging retailers, spider mites, birds making pigs of themselves. Where will it end? Ella, at 94, is a dedicated price-watcher. In April, it was she who kept us informed about the rising cost of maple syrup in Central Canada. She switched to eating raspberry jam on her pancakes and advised us to do the same. Now, with this berry situation, who knows what Ella will try next?

Mid-afternoon. Grandma and the aunts are all making fruit fluffs for the wedding. A trendier cook might call this concoction of fruit, cream and egg white a mousse or even a cold soufflé, but the aunts tell it like it is. A fluff.

"We got sick of squares," declares Grandma, whose strawberry fluff has been a hit at local fetes. "Alice is home right now, making pineapple fluff," she announces. Aunt Bea is threatening to do the same. "There'll be darned few strawberries, you can bet," she tells me.

Early evening. Wedding time. The air is heavy with the scent of sweet clover and wild roses. In the church, farmers with sunburned faces and white foreheads swelter through the service in suits and ties. Later, at the reception, they eye the tall, cool bottles of wine on the tables, but the corkscrew has gone missing. Wisely, the old people haul chairs outside and sit in the shade, waiting patiently. A good dinner is always worth a little waiting.

"There'll be strawberry shortcake for desert," predicts the uncle beside me.

Wrong. It's pineapple fluff.

Here's a menu for the happiest of summer occasions – a small wedding in the garden. This menu is suitable for a small home reception or even a rehearsal dinner the night before. Should you decide on a bigger wedding, just multiply the recipes.

Although this is a wedding feast, it's a small one, and I haven't included the traditional, large wedding cake. If you want one, either the Maple Angel Cake (from the June menu) or the Double Chocolate Carrot Cake (from the April menu) will be wonderful. Simply ice with whipped cream and decorate with fresh garden flowers such as tiny rosebuds, sweet peas, nasturtiums or poppies.

RICOTTA AL FORNO WITH BABY RADISHES

This looks like a large wheel of cheese but tastes like no cheese you've ever eaten. If you don't like olives, other flavors may be introduced – hot pepper, your favorite herbs, shredded smoked salmon and dill. When it cools, this cheese has a firm, pâtélike texture and is delicious with miniature bagels and baby radishes. Serve this as an appetizer on small plates (with forks), while guests are winding down after the ceremony.

2	8 oz (250 g) pkgs ricotta cheese	2
2 tbsp	butter	30 mL
1/4 cup	bread crumbs	50 mL
4	eggs	4
1/2 cup	Parmesan cheese, grated	125 mL
2	cloves garlic, mashed	2
	salt and pepper	
1/2 cup	ripe olives, chopped	125 mL
1/2 cup	stuffed olives, chopped	125 mL
1/2 cup	walnuts, chopped	1/2 cup
	salt and freshly ground pepper	
3	bunches baby radishes with leaves for garnish	3
	miniature bagels	

❖ Ricotta is often a weepy cheese, so drain it first. Double a large piece of cheesecloth, forming a square. Place cheese in the center. Tie opposite ends together to form a hobo bag around the cheese, and hang it over the faucet. It will drain in about 1 hour.

Preheat oven to 375 F (190 C).

Butter a 9 inch (2 L) springform pan. Coat it with bread crumbs and shake off excess crumbs. Mix together ricotta, eggs and

81

continues...

On the Table

For any other barbecue, I'd fling a bright red patchwork quilt on the table and use red and blue bandanas from a discount store for napkins, colorful platters and baskets for serving pieces and a huge bundle of mixed garden flowers. Sunflowers, marigolds and delphiniums make a superb combination, especially in a shiny black vase. But…

Parmesan in a medium bowl and blend with a fork. Stir in garlic. Season lightly with salt, generously with pepper. Pour half the mixture in the pan. Sprinkle cheese with ripe olives, stuffed olives and walnuts. Pour remaining cheese over top.

Bake for 1 hour. Reduce heat to 325 F (160 C) and continue baking 30 minutes longer or until top is firm and lightly golden. Let cool at least 1 hour before removing rim.

Run a knife around the cheese and release the spring. If cheese is still weepy, don't worry, it depends on the composition of your cheese. Allow it to drain onto a platter until it stops weeping.

To serve, line a round, flat basket with leaf lettuce or a linen napkin. Place the cheese (still on the springform base) in the middle. Surround it with washed, trimmed baby radishes that have a bit of green left on top and thinly sliced miniature bagels. Slice into wedges. Serves 12 to 16 as an appetizer.

CHICKEN INDIENNE

This is a delicious, finger-lickin' chicken dish that can either be prepared ahead of time and reheated in the oven or grilled while the party is enjoying the appetizer and drinking the first toasts to the bride and groom. If you do it that way, put a volunteer chef in charge of the chicken, and expect it to take about 45 minutes. The smell of it cooking will be reason enough to celebrate. Leftovers are good cold.

1 1/2 cups	plain yogurt	375 mL
4 tbsp	lemon juice	60 mL
2 tbsp	vegetable oil	30 mL
1 tsp	salt	5 mL
2	garlic cloves, crushed	2
1 tsp	ground cumin	5 mL
2 tsp	curry powder	10 mL
2 tsp	ginger	10 mL
1 tsp	almond extract	5 mL
6 lbs	chicken legs and breasts	3.5 kg

❖ In a large container, mix together yogurt, lemon juice, oil, spices and almond extract. Wash chicken parts and pat dry. Place in yogurt mixture and turn, so they're well covered. Cover container and refrigerate about 2 hours.

Remove chicken, reserving the marinade. Place chicken on an oiled grill, bone-side down, 6 inches (15 cm) from medium-hot coals. Put the lid down on the barbecue (or cover with a roaster lid) and grill 20 minutes. Turn chicken, brush with marinade and cover to finish grilling, basting several times as it cooks. This will take about 25 minutes longer. Cut a small slit in the meatiest part of the chicken to see if the juices run clear – chicken should not be served rare.

Serves 12 to 14.

…for a wedding, use a pastel cloth, either pink, yellow or whatever shade the bride loves most. If you don't have such a cloth, buy inexpensive cotton. Arrange a bundle of garden flowers in complementary shades in the middle of the table. When it's time for dessert, arrange it on a smaller table with glasses for the champagne toast.

GARDEN FRITATTAS WITH WILD MUSHROOMS

These are thick, flavorful omelettes intended to be served cool or at room temperature. Dried wild mushrooms give this dish an earthy flavor and meaty texture that are quite delicious. Either boletes or porcini may be used. Make the fritattas in the morning and refrigerate, covered, until about 1 hour before serving. Each fritatta will serve 6.

2	3/8 oz (10 g) pkgs dried bolete mushrooms, soaked	2
6	medium fresh white mushrooms, sliced	6
1	green onion, diced	1
2 tbsp	oil	30 mL
1	garlic clove, peeled and minced	1
	coarse salt and freshly ground pepper	
8	eggs	8
1/4 cup	Parmesan cheese, grated	50 mL
1/2 cup	fresh parsley, coarsely chopped	125 mL
3	slices back bacon, diced	3
2 tbsp	butter	30 mL
	tomatoes	
	cucumbers	
	springs of parsley for garnish	

❖ Soak mushrooms in cold water until soft and pliable. Rinse in a fine sieve until water runs clear (to remove sand). Drain. Slice all mushrooms. Heat oil in a medium saucepan. Sauté garlic briefly, but don't let it brown. Add mushrooms and onion, and sauté briefly until onion is transparent. Season with salt and pepper. Set aside to cool.

Beat eggs with a fork. Add Parmesan, parsley, bacon and mushrooms. Wipe a medium frying pan with oil, then melt butter. Add egg mixture. Lower heat and cook until eggs are nearly set and edges are firm. Carefully slide out of the frying pan onto a plate and then invert back into pan. (You may want to wipe the pan with a little more oil.) Cook briefly and slide onto a large round serving plate. Cover and refrigerate until 1 hour before serving.

Just before serving, cut the fritattas into wedges and surround with sliced tomatoes, cucumbers and sprigs of parsley or other garden herbs.

Serves 6. To serve a crowd, make more fritattas. This is a great picnic dish, so save the leftovers for later.

COOK'S NOTE: The fritatta is one of the world's most versatile and forgiving dishes. If wild mushrooms are not available, substitute any vegetable you wish – green peas, chopped cooked artichoke hearts, green beans, diced cooked carrots. Add cheese if you like.

In the Bottle

Any fruity and crisp white is fine with grilled chicken. If you want a wine that will make a statement in its own right and invite the vegetables and the cheese to complement it, a cooled bottle of Vino Nobile de Montepulciano will be fine. So will Verdicchio dei Castelli di Jesi, a wonderfully distinctive Italian white with strong fruit and vegetal flavors. Asti-spumante, virtually iced, is a fine option for the toasts.

THAI RICE SALAD WITH LIME VINAIGRETTE

This Thai recipe adapts easily to any party, especially a summer buffet. Do not be dismayed by the lengthy ingredient list – this crowd-pleasing salad is worth it. Note: Other herbs may be substituted, but whatever you use must be fresh.

VINAIGRETTE

3/4 cup	good olive oil	175 mL
1/2 cup	canola oil	125 mL
1/2 cup	balsamic vinegar	125 mL
1/4 cup	lime juice, freshly squeezed	50 mL
1 tsp	lime rind, grated	5 mL
8	green onions, including green tops, minced	8
3/4 cup	fresh parsley, chopped	175 mL
1	clove garlic, minced	1
2 tsp	granulated sugar	10 mL
	salt and pepper	

SALAD

2 cups	long-grain brown rice	500 mL
2 cups	long-grain white rice	500 mL
6	green onions, including green tops, finely chopped	6
1 cup	fresh parsley, minced	250 mL
1/2 cup	fresh basil, chopped	125 mL
1/2 cup	fresh cilantro, chopped	125 mL
1/4 cup	fresh mint, chopped	50 mL
1 cup	frozen tiny green peas	250 mL
	shredded iceberg lettuce	
	green onion tops, fresh herb sprigs, chive blossoms (if available) for garnish	

❖ To make the vinaigrette, combine all ingredients in a jar and shake well. Reserve.

Cook brown rice as directed on the package. Fluff with a fork and transfer to a large mixing bowl. Cook white rice as directed on package. Fluff with a fork, then add to brown rice.

Toss warm rice with about one-third of the vinaigrette. Fluff rice frequently until it cools completely, then cover and let stand at room temperature for several hours or as long as overnight.

Toss with green onions, herbs, green peas and remaining vinaigrette to taste. Let stand about 30 minutes for flavors to blend. Peas will thaw sufficiently.

Serve on a platter, mounding the rice salad on a bed of shredded lettuce. Garnish with long shreds of green onion, sprigs of fresh herbs and chive blossoms. Tuck additional chive blossoms around the bottom.

Serves 12 to 16.

RHUBARB BERRY CUSTARD PIE

I make this when I have lots of fresh berries. Virtually any berry will do, but a mixture of strawberries and blueberries is an inspired combination. If you make it in the autumn, cranberries are excellent with it, but do add a wisp more sugar.

Why a pie for a wedding feast? Because it's summer, it's delicious, and your guests will lick their plates.

Pastry to line a 9 x 13 inch (4 L) baking pan.

FILLING

6 cups	rhubarb, diced	1 1/2 L
1 cup	mixed berries	250 mL
1 1/2 cups	white sugar	375 mL
1 tsp	cinnamon	5 mL
1/3 cup	flour	75 mL
1 cup	skim milk yogurt	250 mL
4	eggs	4

TOPPING

1/2 cup	flour	125 mL
1/2 cup	brown sugar	125 mL
1/4 cup	soft butter	50 mL

❖   Preheat oven to 450 F (230 C).

Pour diced rhubarb into unbaked pastry shell. Sprinkle randomly with berries. Mix together sugar, cinnamon and flour. With a wire whisk, beat in yogurt and eggs. Pour mixture evenly over rhubarb.

Blend topping ingredients until crumbly. Sprinkle over fruit. Bake 15 minutes, then reduce heat to 325 F (160 C) for 35 to 40 minutes until fruit is tender and custard is lightly set. Let cool about 30 minutes before serving. Serve warm or cold with ice cream. Serves 8.

COOK'S NOTE: For this party, bake two pies, using a different combination of berries in each. Garnish with fresh berries and sprigs of mint if you wish.

PEANUT BUTTER WEDDING COOKIES WITH WHITE CHOCOLATE GLAZE

This is a family wedding, and what could be more family than peanut butter cookies?

COOKIES

1 cup	vegetable shortening	250 mL
1/3 cup	butter	75 mL
1 cup	chunky peanut butter	250 mL
1 cup	brown sugar, packed	250 mL
1 cup	white sugar	250 mL
2	eggs	2
2 tsp	vanilla	10 mL
2 1/2 cups	flour	625 mL
1 tsp	baking soda	5 mL
1/4 tsp	salt	1 mL

GLAZE

1 cup	white chocolate pieces	250 mL
2 tbsp	butter	50 mL
1 tbsp	honey	15 mL
1 tsp	instant coffee powder	5 mL

❖ Preheat oven to 350 F (180 C).

In a bowl, beat together shortening, butter, peanut butter, sugars, eggs and vanilla. In another bowl, stir together flour, baking soda and salt. Add to creamed mixture gradually, beating at low speed to blend well. Chill 20 minutes.

Shape dough into 1/2 inch (1.5 cm) balls and place on ungreased baking sheets. Bake 8 to 10 minutes or until cookies flatten slightly and are firm to the touch. Cool slightly, then remove to a cooling rack. Drizzle with white chocolate glaze. Makes about 10 dozen small cookies. (To make a larger, child-approved cookie, make the dough balls twice as big and bake a little longer.)

Melt white chocolate pieces over hot (not boiling) water. Stir in butter, honey and instant coffee powder. Drizzle over cooled cookies.

ICED TEA WITH MINT AND LIME

Black currant tea has a romantic, slightly resinous aroma that reminds me of Christmas trees. It makes the best iced tea.

6	black currant tea bags	6
4 cups	boiling water	1 L
2 tbsp	fresh mint, chopped	25 mL
1/2 cup	sugar (or more to taste)	125 mL
1 cup	cold water	250 mL
1/2 cup	lemon juice	125 mL
1/2 cup	lime juice	125 mL
	mint leaves, lemon and lime slices for garnish	

❖ Pour boiling water over tea bags and mint. Cover and let steep 5 minutes. Strain and stir in sugar until dissolved. Add cold water and lemon and lime juices.

To serve, pour in ice-filled glasses and garnish with lemon and mint.

Makes about 8 servings over ice.

ORANGE RHUBARB SPRITZERS

Make the rhubarb juice ahead of time. It's delicious straight or mixed in this spritzer.

JUICE

8 cups	rhubarb, diced	2 L
1	orange, sliced	1
3	cinnamon sticks	3
1 gallon	water	4 L
1 cup	sugar	250 mL

❖ Put rhubarb, orange slices, cinnamon sticks, water and sugar in a large nonmetal saucepan and bring to a boil. Reduce heat to simmer, and cook 30 minutes.

Remove from heat. Strain juice through cheesecloth and discard pulp. Return juice to the pan and bring back to a boil. Cook briefly, cool and pour in large bottles. Makes about 1 gallon (4 L).

SPRITZERS

1/2 cup	rhubarb juice	125 mL
1/4 cup	orange juice, freshly squeezed	50 mL
	ice cubes	
	soda water	
	orange twist	
	mint leaves	

❖ Pour rhubarb juice and orange juice over ice in a tall glass. Add a twist of orange. Top up with soda water and stuff a generous sprig of mint in the glass, squashing it so the aroma is released. Straws are a good idea with spritzers – they keep the ice cubes and foliage away from your nose. Each spritzer serves 1.

COOK'S NOTE: To turn this recipe into a punch, simply mix the rhubarb and orange juices in a 2-to-1 proportion and add soda water, gingerale or sparkling wine to taste.

A Little Romance

Consider: Somewhere today there may be two people cuddled together on an iceberg, feeding each other nibbles of frozen fish. If they're in love, nectar and ambrosia could not be sweeter.

Give them a year, and the same two people may be seated at a table in Le Canard Mort, fighting tooth and claw and being hateful to each other over $200 worth of oysters and champagne. It will not be a romantic meal, in spite of all that chefs, waiters, subtle lighting and, God knows, oysters can do.

That's the tricky bit about romantic meals. They aren't just about what or where – they're mostly about whom.

They're also about how much. According to my research, passion does not feed on vast slabs of prime rib and lashings of gravy. People who are mad about each other often lose the desire to eat, which cannot be good news for the restaurant business.

In fact, most of what's been written about romantic dinners and how to cook them is impossibly long and involved. When you're in love, cooking and eating should be an easy, relaxed time, with lots of touching and laughing.

Remember that great, lusty eating scene in the movie version of Tom Jones? There was Tom, grabbing a joint of venison in both hands, tearing at it with his strong, white teeth, feeding bites to the luscious Widow Waters. And there was the Widow, loving every messy morsel and to heck with her expensive dress.

*Grilled Cheese and Roasted
Peppers in Vine Leaves*

Hoisin-Grilled Lamb Filets

*Gingered Peaches with
Nasturtium Blossoms*

Raspberry Cream Brule

Iced Coffee with Brandy

THE AFTERMATH

*Heartbreak Cookies
with Lottsa Chocolate*

People have been seduced by everything from rare white truffles to a Mars Bar and in every season from typhoons to blizzards.

But for my money, the most seductive times are hot August nights with the scent of a hundred flowers in the air and the breeze barely bending the candle flame.

Here's a simple feast for two people. You'll need a knife for the grilled cheese, forks for the peaches and a spoon for the dessert. Other than that, it's all a matter of hands.

This feast is entirely portable. Both the appetizer and the main course can easily be grilled on a small hibachi or one of those picnic-type barbecues that show up in the sylvan glades of our better parks. Be sure to take along some coals and barbecue starter, and don't forget a blanket and the mosquito coil.

GRILLED CHEESE AND ROASTED PEPPERS
IN VINE LEAVES

Buy mild, snow goat cheese or fresh mozzarella for this meal. An aged goat cheese will be too assertive, and an inferior mozzarella will be like melted rubber. You can roast your own peppers (see Tapenade of Roasted Peppers and Sun-Dried Tomatoes, January menu), but I take the easy route and use canned roasted red peppers, packed in oil or water, available in any Italian market.

6	canned grape vine leaves	6
2	small fresh goat cheeses	2
2 tbsp	sweet red peppers, roasted and chopped	30 mL
	toasted baguette, sliced	
	olive oil	

❖ Unroll grape vine leaves, and rinse well in cold water. Pat dry on both sides. Using three leaves per package, lay them one on top of the other and center the cheese on the leaves. Spoon peppers on top and wrap cheese snugly, tying each package with household string. (This may not be necessary, but it saves the odd disaster.)

Brush the grill with oil, and grill cheese packages about 5 minutes per side. If cheese should begin to leak copiously before 5 minutes are up, consider it done and move that package off the fire.

Meanwhile, brush baguette slices with olive oil and toast over grill until golden brown.

To serve, open the cheese packages and spread melted cheese and peppers on toasted baguette slices. Serves 2.

COOK'S NOTE: This easy, unusual and utterly delicious appetizer for a barbecue can be done for many people at one time. But your guests need to be seated to enjoy it – this is definitely not for the standard cocktail party juggling act.

HOISIN-GRILLED LAMB FILETS

Lamb filets are so small and tender that two per person is about right. I use the frozen ones from New Zealand because they're readily available and the quality is good. If you don't like lamb, or can't find the filets, pork tenderloin makes an excellent substitute. Buy about an 8 oz (250 g) piece, and slice it into quarters lengthwise.

Either pita bread or soft flour tortillas will work well in this dish.

	olive oil	
4	lamb fillets	4
1/4 cup	hoisin sauce	50 mL
4	lettuce leaves	4
	soft leaf lettuce (oak leaf, red leaf, butter or Grand Rapids leaf)	
2	green onions, shredded lengthwise	2
	fresh cilantro sprigs	
2	pitas or tortillas	2

❖ Brush grill with oil.

Grill meat over hot coals about 5 minutes. Turn and brush with hoisin sauce. Grill about five minutes more or until done to taste. Brush the other side with hoisin sauce.

Meanwhile, brush pita bread or tortillas with olive oil and warm over the grill.

To serve, place a lettuce leaf on the warmed bread. Put two strips of meat on the lettuce, add shredded green onion and cilantro sprigs, and roll the bread around it. Enjoy. Serves 2.

Cook's Note: Some people have small appetites, especially when they're besotted and don't want to take all night eating. If a whole pita is too much bread for your taste, cut it in half and stuff it with the lettuce, meat and fixin's. In that case, one pita will serve two, but I wouldn't count on it.

GINGERED PEACH SALAD WITH NASTURTIUM BLOSSOMS

The cool sweet flesh of peaches is exactly what Cupid ordered with lamb. Buy them a day ahead and leave them in an open bowl overnight, just so you can enjoy the seductive aroma of ripening peaches in the morning. If the peaches aren't perfect when you shop, use nectarines instead. You won't even have to peel them.

2	ripe peaches, peeled and sliced	2
1 tbsp	lemon juice	15 mL
1/2 tsp	lemon rind, finely grated	2 mL
1 tbsp	sugar	15 mL
1/4 tsp	salt	1 mL
	black pepper, freshly ground	
1/4 tsp	cumin	1 mL
1 tsp	curry powder	5 mL
1 tsp	ginger, freshly grated	5 mL
1 tsp	bland salad oil	5 mL
6	mint leaves, minced	6
	nasturtium blossoms for garnish	

❖ Lay sliced peaches in a glass bowl, and immediately pour lemon juice and rind on them, turning gently. (The lemon juice will keep them from discoloring.)

Put all other ingredients in a small jar and shake to combine. Pour over peaches and refrigerate, covered, about 1 hour.

Bring to room temperature before serving so the fragrance of the dish will be released. Serve on a small platter or in a pretty, shallow bowl garnished with nasturtium blossoms. Serves 2.

COOK'S NOTE: If you have red nasturtiums, shred a couple of blossoms and sprinkle them over the peaches. They add a peppery flavor and the color is absolutely electric.

On the Table

Keep it informal. Have as many candles as you wish – a single fat candle or a whole passle. A low bowl of lush cabbage roses are lovely on the table, especially on a warm evening when the scent is intensely sensual. So is a single flower. Or none. This is one dining experience that doesn't depend on trappings.

In the Bottle

A wonderful red sets off the lamb with proper romantic flourish. Hoisin sauce is sweet and earthy, but the dimension it adds to meat will enhance dense flavors. Cabernet franc or merlot is a good choice, as is a Barbera or a Dolcetto d'Alba. A particularly ripe and semimature red zinfandel is…

RASPBERRY CREAM BRULE

2 cups	ripe raspberries	500 mL
1/2 cup	sour cream	125 mL
2 tsp	granulated sugar	10 mL
1 tsp	vanilla	5 mL
2 tsp	brown sugar	10 mL

❖ Put berries in two heatproof dishes.

Sweeten sour cream with granulated sugar and stir in vanilla. Divide sour cream between the two dishes. Sprinkle with brown sugar. Place under the broiler just until sugar melts and cream begins to bubble and brown slightly.

Serve immediately. Serves 2.

COOK'S NOTE: If you decide to make it a picnic, just fold the berries into the cream, white sugar and vanilla. Sprinkle with brown sugar just before you eat and forget broiling. They'll be delicious this way, especially if you have a few extra berries to fling over the top.

ICED COFFEE WITH BRANDY

The Oriental Hotel in Bangkok serves the world's best iced coffee, and the waitresses make it with such panache that it's worth ordering just for the ceremony. Still, I longed for a slosh of brandy in it. Be sure the coffee is strong.

Arrange a special tray for this – snifters straight from the freezer, ice cubes and tongs in a frosted bowl, small pitchers with syrup and cream, and of course the best bottle of brandy you can lay your hands on.

2 cups	European roast coffee	500 mL
1/2 cup	brandy	125 mL
	ice cubes	
	light corn syrup	
	coffee cream	

❖   Make the coffee ahead of time and refrigerate.

Put ice cubes in the snifters. Pour brandy over the cubes, then coffee. Add corn syrup to taste, then cream. (I like watching the cream swirl into the dark liquid. It always reminds me of smoke.) Enjoy. Serves 2.

COOK'S NOTE: If you're a cook who thinks ahead, think about freezing strong coffee in ice cubes. They're handy for any iced coffee, and if you run them through an ice crusher and drizzle a little brandy over top, they make a super shave ice.

…perfect. For something dramatic and different, an Alsatian Riesling of good vintage and provenance is a stunning foil. A glass of ice-cold Marsala enhances and intensifies the taste of cream brule, and it's assertive enough to stand up to berries.

THE AFTERMATH

Ah, but we all know the path to romance is riddled with potholes, don't we? Falling in love is hell, as anybody over the age of eleven can attest. Can't eat, can't sleep, can't concentrate. Endless waiting for the phone to ring, and when it does, the adrenalin crashes through your veins, your heart thumps and bangs, your ribs hurt and your voice goes squeaky. You can't breathe. You run around with a silly grin on your face and everybody thinks you're dotty. And then the beloved voice on the other end tells you his goldfish is sick so he can't see you tonight, at which point you want to die.

All this is only temporary, of course, but it's hard to be reasonable while you're crying into your third martini.

Eating something you shouldn't will help. Chocolate is good in an emergency, or so I've always found. Huge chocolate cookies work well; even thumping the dough together has a certain therapeutic effect.

Baking them feels good. Eating them feels better. Break one in half while it's still warm – the white chocolate chunks are melty, pully as warm cheese, soft as silk on the tongue. Never mind the calories. If they keep you out of the gin bottle, they're well spent.

HEARTBREAK COOKIES WITH LOTTSA CHOCOLATE

These are similar to my favorite cookies from the Cookies By George people. No matter how lousy I feel, these improve the situation.

1 cup	butter	250 mL
2 cups	granulated sugar	500 mL
2	eggs	2
2 tsp	vanilla	10 mL
1 1/2 cups	all-purpose flour	375 mL
1 cup	cocoa	250 mL
1 tsp	baking powder	5 mL
1 tsp	salt	5 mL
1 cup	white chocolate chunks	250 mL
1/2 cup	almonds, chopped	125 mL

❖ Preheat oven to 350 F (180 C).

Cream butter and sugar. Beat in eggs and vanilla. In a separate bowl, stir together flour, cocoa, baking powder and salt. Stir about half the flour mixture in the creamed mixture. Stir in white chocolate, nuts and remaining flour mixture.

Drop by tablespoons (15 mL) on lightly greased baking sheets. Bake 10 to 12 minutes or until just firm but still springy to the touch. Cookies will be soft but will firm up when cooled. Let cool 5 minutes before removing to wire racks. Makes about 30 cookies.

Tray Bon

One winter when I was a little kid, my grandmother moved in with us.

For eighty-odd years she'd been as independent as quack grass, but eventually her body decided to call it quits. She was diabetic and had a tricky heart. She'd shrunk too, and her bones brittled, as bones do in old age.

At first she'd been a presence in the kitchen, cooking, stewing, making terrific chicken noodle soup. But the day came when she could no longer see to whack up the bird, and soon Grandma spent less time in the kitchen and more upstairs in her room. Finally, she began eating all her meals on a tray.

In spite of that, she always wore an apron with a bib and two big pockets, as though expecting to be called back to the stoves at any moment. Grandma's apron was her uniform and maybe her armor. As the most frequent tray bearer, I noticed that she never ate unless she was wearing it.

Apart from being a good cook and a good listener, Grandma had another outstanding quality: she was terrific at minding her own business. It was one of the reasons why I spent so much time in her room. When Lexie Headington didn't invite me to her party, or somebody called me a sissy frogface Frenchman, I would scoot under my mother's all-seeing eye, hide in Grandma's room and howl with impunity.

NINE

SEPTEMBER

BREAKFAST TRAY MENU

Orange Flower Cocktail

Omelet Soufflé

Plum Sauce

Croissants

Coffee

AFTERNOON TEA TRAY MENU

Quick Cheddar Bacon Scones

Lemon Blueberry Muffins

Orange Date Loaf with Orange Cream Cheese

Earl Grey Tea

That's where I went the day I found Tim, my big orange cat, frozen stiff behind the garage, awaiting spring thaw and a decent burial. Tim's untimely death had already been mourned by every member of the family, and a replacement cat named Tiger was already in residence. But all that winter, in the blue-snow afternoons between school and supper, I would stand among the frozen cabbages, blubbering over my dead cat until my nose began to drip. Then I'd run to Grandma's room where private grief was respected, and I could snivel all I wanted and not say why. Life was cruel, and Grandma knew it.

In spite of her exile upstairs, she was a sociable person, and Saturday afternoons, Grandma received. Usually it was just fat Mrs. Sayer, who had legs like stove pipes, and huffed and puffed all the way upstairs, so I'd go with her and hang around, listening for hot gossip, until Mom called me to get the tray.

Mom was good at tea trays. She had an endless supply of hand-embroidered teacloths, and on Saturday she fussed with the best cups, and got out the sugar lumps instead of the plain, granulated kind we used the rest of the time. She wasn't into tea sandwiches, which were considered too fiddley for anything but weddings, but she made big muffins and terrific date loaf, sweetened with orange juice so Gram could eat it. Her baking powder scones were legendary. She'd pile them on the plate while they were still hot, with the butter melting in little yellow puddles, a blob of homemade grape jelly on each and more jelly on the side.

Gram couldn't eat the jelly, and she'd fold her lips into a thin, tight line while she watched fat Mrs. Sayer wolfing it down.

Gram hated missing out on all the sweets. One Sunday night when she thought we were all at church, I found her downstairs in the kitchen attacking a jar of strawberry jam with a big spoon. Caught red-handed, she was furious and not about to apologize.

"Getting old is no fun," she snapped, slamming the lid onto the jar so hard I figured we'd never get it off again.

"Help me upstairs," she said. "And don't you dare tell your Mother."

I didn't.

The following menus are downscaled to fit a tray. Trays in bed are the ultimate luxury, but afternoon trays laden with tea and scrumptious tidbits can be intimate, comforting meals, just right for friendly confidences over the teacups.

MORNING TRAY FOOD

Man is seldom at his world-conquering best as dawn breaks. Neither is woman.

If I had my way, those hours between six and ten a.m. would be reserved for small children and hamsters (who have been up all night anyway). They could mess around the kitchen with a box of Fruit Loops, spilling and slopping with abandon, until 10 o'clock, when Mr. Clean would arrive. He'd zap the mess, stuff the hamster back in its cage and drop the child at Aunt Mabel's Day Care and Bagel Shop.

The rest of us would sleep until eleven.

Alack, the world is not unfolding as it should.

The only route to morning decadence is a tray in bed. It's a given that somebody else should do the cooking, make the coffee and toddle out to the mailbox to get the Sunday paper.

After all, if you have to leave your warm bed, go all the way to the kitchen, cook this and that and lug it all back, where's the fun? By that time the dog will want out, then he'll want his breakfast, then the kids will be up. The thing to do is stay in bed and feign sleep, having pinned a recipe to the opposite pillow just after midnight.

ORANGE FLOWER COCKTAIL

This lovely eye-opener looks like the juice of Italian blood oranges and has an elusive fragrance, courtesy of the best French orange flower water. (It's in the blue bottle with flowers all over the label.)

1 cup	orange juice, freshly squeezed	250 mL
1 cup	cranberry cocktail	250 mL
4 tsp	orange flower water	20 mL
2 tsp	liquid honey	10 mL
	mint leaves for garnish	

❖ In a blender, whiz together juice, cranberry cocktail, orange flower water and honey. Pour in tall, stemmed glasses. Garnish with mint leaves. Serves 2, with refills.

OMELET SOUFFLÉ

If you've been very deserving, you could request toast with this, but a couple of lovely croissants, warmed while the soufflé rises, will be even better.

4	eggs, separated	4
1 tbsp	flour	15 mL
1 tsp	vanilla extract	5 mL
1 tsp	lemon juice	5 mL
1/2 cup	sugar	125 mL
	plum sauce	

❖ Preheat oven to 350 F (180 C).

Beat egg yolks with flour, vanilla and lemon juice. In a separate bowl, beat egg whites until foamy. Add sugar and beat until stiff. Fold egg whites into egg yolk mixture.

Butter a gratin dish or pie plate and spread about 1 cup (250 mL) of Plum Sauce in the bottom. Spoon the egg mixture on top.

Bake in preheated oven 15 to 20 minutes, until puffed and golden. Serve with remaining Plum Sauce drizzled over the top. Serves 2.

PLUM SAUCE

Nectarines can be substituted, or you can go half and half. Do not peel the plums – the skins add color, flavor and texture.

2 cups	blue plums, quartered	50 mL
1/2 cup	sugar	125 mL
1 tsp	ginger, freshly grated	5 mL
1/2 tsp	cinnamon	2 mL

❖ Put all ingredients in a small saucepan and simmer about 10 minutes, until plums are tender. Makes about 1 1/2 cups (375 mL).

AFTERNOON TEA TRAY

QUICK CHEDDAR BACON SCONES

Serve these with butter and a small scoop of grape jelly or rhubarb chutney. Yum. A few tiny gherkins on the side won't hurt.

3 cups	biscuit mix	750 mL
2 tbsp	granulated sugar	30 mL
1/2 cup	Cheddar cheese, grated	125 mL
2	slices bacon	2
1 cup	water	250 mL
1	egg	1

❖ Preheat oven to 425 F (220 C).

Fry bacon until crisp, drain and dice.

Combine biscuit mix, sugar, cheese and bacon in a large bowl. Beat together water and egg. Make a well in the dry ingredients and add the liquid. Stir only until a soft dough forms.

Turn dough onto a floured board and knead briefly, no more than 10 times. Form into a round loaf. Place on an ungreased baking sheet and mark the top in 8 sections. Bake about 12 to 15 minutes or until golden brown. Makes 8 large scones.

On the Table

The breakfast tray needs a single blossom in a bud vase. Nothing wrong with a half-opened rose. For the afternoon tray, break out the delicate china, the hand-embroidered tray cloth, the fine linen napkins you never expected to use. If pansies or asters are left in the garden, tuck a few in a small jug. Sprigs of wild goldenrod and purple asters are lovely too. Don't worry about decorating the midnight tray. Just turn your electric blanket up to nine and enjoy.

LEMON BLUEBERRY MUFFINS

To heck with modesty – these are quite likely the world's best blueberry muffins. Use skim milk yogurt to save calories.

2	eggs	2
1/2 cup	brown sugar	125 mL
1/3 cup	vegetable oil	75 mL
1 tbsp	lemon juice	15 mL
1 cup	yogurt	250 mL
2 cups	flour	500 mL
1 tbsp	baking powder	15 mL
1/2 cup	walnuts, chopped	125 mL
1 cup	frozen blueberries	250 mL
1 tsp	lemon rind, grated	5 mL

❖ Preheat oven to 400 F (200 C).

In a bowl, beat eggs, sugar, oil, lemon juice and yogurt until well blended.

In another bowl, sift together flour and baking powder. Add egg mixture and stir just enough to blend ingredients. Fold in nuts, frozen berries and lemon rind. Pour into greased and floured muffin tins. Bake 18 to 20 minutes until golden. Makes about 1 dozen big muffins.

MOM'S ORANGE DATE LOAF

This is good when it's barely cool, but it tastes even better the next day, or the day after that, when the dates have had a chance to get acquainted with the orange.

1/4 cup	butter	50 mL
3/4 cup	granulated sugar	175 mL
2 tbsp	orange rind	30 mL
1 cup	orange juice	250 mL
3	eggs	3
1 cup	pitted dates, chopped	250 mL
2 cups	flour	550 mL
1/2 cup	bran cereal	125 mL
2 1/2 tsp	baking powder	12 mL
1/2 tsp	baking soda	2 mL
1/2 tsp	salt	2 mL

❖ Preheat oven to 350 F (180 C).

Grease and flour a 9 x 5 inch (2 L) loaf pan.

Cream together butter and sugar in a large bowl. Beat in eggs, orange juice and rind.

Toss dates with 1/4 cup (50 mL) of flour so they won't stick together or sink to the bottom of the loaf. Stir together remaining flour, bran cereal (bran buds or bran flakes), baking powder, soda and salt. Add to creamed mixture and stir just until mixed. Stir in floured dates and spoon into pan. Bake about 1 hour or until a tester inserted in the middle comes out clean. Let cool 10 minutes in the pan. Remove from the pan and let cool completely on a wire rack before slicing. Spread slices with Orange Cream Cheese. Makes 1 loaf.

In the Bottle

Wine with tea? Why not? A fragrant Mosel is fine on the afternoon tray, as is a robust, sapid Rheinpfalz made from a grape like Kerner or Ortega. Nothing can be better than iced champagne on the breakfast tray – a half bottle, though, because you don't want to lose all perspective…

ORANGE CREAM CHEESE

Not essential, but it's so good on the date bread.

1 cup	light cream cheese	250 mL
1/2 tsp	orange rind, grated	2 mL
1 tbsp	orange marmalade	15 mL

❖ Soften cream cheese by bringing it to room temperature. Beat in orange rind and marmalade. (If marmalade peel is coarse, chop it.)

MIDNIGHT TRAY FOOD

Sooner or later, it comes to all of us. The blues. The deep, dark funk. Misery.

A sudden visit from the taxman can bring it on. So can a faithless lover or a lost job. Or maybe it's just your turn to hit the emotional skids. Whatever it is, you can't sleep for fretting. A midnight snack is in order.

The tray should be small. It only needs room for one plate and one mug. I like milky, foamy coffee with this, or if I'm completely down, hot chocolate. Other people can't deal with misery unless they have a pot of tea or milk on the side. Whatever it takes, go for it.

TOTI'S WALNUT TOAST

Toti is an artist who lives in a parklike setting on Vancouver Island. Along with her friendship and several of her etchings, I treasure her recipe for walnut toast. She makes it for breakfast, but I like it at night.

2	slices French bread, buttered	2
1/2 cup	walnuts, chopped	125 mL
2 tbsp	brown sugar	30 mL

❖ Divide walnuts between bread slices, patting them into butter. Sprinkle generously with brown sugar. Broil about 4 inches (9.5 cm) from the heat until sugar bubbles. Eat immediately.

…on the day. With walnut toast in bed at midnight, you might have a glass of port. If by wonderful chance you're with someone you're particularly fond of, forget the mocha, drink champagne, start feeding each other and pretend it's a rainy night in Paris.

The Year We Raised Turkeys

The year we raised turkeys, I seriously considered becoming a vegetarian.

There were eight of us involved in this back-to-the-land gesture, and I suppose we saw it as a serious communal effort to raise our own food and take the pressure off the starving millions. The only one of the group who knew beans about livestock was my husband, Ed, who was raised on a farm and should have known better. But when someone offered us a small flock of chicks, free of charge, I was as gullible as the rest of them.

To begin with, my definition of a small flock of chickens ran to a dozen birds, two dozen at the most. I had not counted on four hundred chickens tearing around my ankles, demanding food. Nor had I counted on the four pigs and sixty turkeys that showed up with them, and a noisy, smelly, cantankerous lot they were too. Someone told me there were also two steers involved in the operation, but I never met them and no beef arrived for my freezer, so they may have been a nasty rumor.

In the end, the pigs were a disappointment. One of them died on the way to the market, forcing the price of bacon up by twenty-five percent. Ed told me the pig's sudden demise was painless and had been brought on by soft living.

It was the turkeys that gave us real trouble. They grew long of wing and leg, but for some reason they stubbornly refused to put on meat, though we fed and watered them nightly and dosed them with turkey starter, vitamins and antibiotics. I voted against the antibiotics, but Ed assured me that turkeys were susceptible to every disease known to man or bird, and without medication they'd come down with some unpronounceable turkey ailment, and none of them would make it to Thanksgiving dinner.

Not only did our turkeys refuse to plump up the way potential Thanksgiving dinners should, but they were the meanest, most evil-tempered birds I had ever met. Our youngest son, Kurt, was a toddler at the time, and the turkeys' great pleasure in life was to chase him, squawking and pecking at his heels, until he stumbled and fell and had to be rescued, wailing, from some particularly vile part of the pen.

Ed finally admitted that he didn't hold them in any sort of esteem. "This bird is stupid," he said, gloomily extracting a furious turkey from a mud puddle. "It will fall in the creek and drown. Or it will find a rain spout, sit under it and end up with pneumonia a week before Thanksgiving. Turkeys are suicidal."

We kept the birds until the end of September. It was a Sunday, and it dawned warm and golden, the sort of end-of-summer day when it feels good to be alive. I felt a little pang at what we were about to do, but Ed pointed out that our flock had enjoyed a full season of bug hunting and brawling around the yard, had a good dinner every day of their lives and had been comfortably housed, with all their medical needs attended to. Unless I wanted four hundred overgrown chickens as house pets, there was nothing to do but get on with it.

I wasn't part of the execution squad. Instead, I drove back and forth with trunkloads of fresh bird corpses to be fast-frozen, and by day's end my freezer was full. I felt that the whole project had been a stroke of genius.

Then came Thanksgiving. When we brought our bird up to the kitchen, it seemed a bit bonier than I remembered. Emaciated is how it looked. We decided that two birds would be a better idea all around.

For some reason both turkeys had many dark blue pin feathers that no amount of careful scrubbing could remove, and they gave an odd greenish-black color to the skin. Although the roasting birds smelled wonderful, I was beginning to have doubts.

When both birds had been loaded aboard my second-smallest platter, there still seemed to be a lot of room left, and the bones stuck out at odd angles, even with the forest of parsley that I distributed in all the worst places.

My mother looked at the turkeys and gave a little sniff. Then she looked at Ed as though he had done her only daughter a great wrong. "Next year I'll bring my own turkey," she snapped. And she did.

The October menu is one that fits as easily into November or December – a family feast that celebrates the traditions of our waning year: the harvest, the cooler days, the longer nights. The roasted bird, the warm spices of autumn, the corn and turnips, are all part of it. I like to start this meal with something to whet the appetite before the main event – thus the focaccia.

FOCACCIA STRIPS WITH ASIAGO AND BACON

Serve these delicious appetizer sandwiches with a glass of dry sherry.

1 recipe	focaccia dough (see Red Onion Focaccia, January menu)	1 recipe
1 tsp	rosemary	5 mL
1 tsp	coarse salt	5 mL
4	strips bacon, diced	4
1	small onion, diced	1
1/4 lb	aged Asiago cheese	125 g

❖ Make the focaccia according to the January recipe, but do not make the red onion topping. Instead, liberally brush the surface of the flatbread with olive oil. Using fingertips, poke indents all over the dough. Sprinkle with coarse salt and rosemary, and bake according to recipe directions. (If you prefer, use less salt.)

While bread is still warm, place on a bread board and slit horizontally, using a sharp, serrated-edge bread knife. Carefully remove top layer.

Quickly fry bacon and onion in a small frying pan. With a truffle or other slicer, cut cheese into the thinnest possible chips. Lay them on the bottom half of the focaccia. Spoon onions, bacon and some of the drippings over cheese and immediately put the top back on. Press lightly.

Using a sharp chef's knife, slice filled focaccia into strips, roughly 2 x 3 inches (5 x 7 cm). Serve while still warm. Serves 10 to 12.

COOK'S NOTE: May be made ahead, wrapped snugly in foil and reheated.

SWEET PEPPER SOUP WITH GALLIANO

I love the full, sweet flavor of red bell peppers with the hint of anise that comes from the fennel and Galliano.

1	medium onion, chopped	1
1	fennel bulb, chopped	1
3	cloves garlic, minced	3
1	medium carrot, finely diced	1
2 tbsp	oil	30 mL
4	sweet red peppers, chopped	4
2 cups	thick tomato sauce	500 mL
4 cups	chicken stock	1 L
	salt and pepper	
	juice of 1 lemon	
1/4 cup	Galliano liqueur	50 mL
	sour cream	
	sprigs of fennel leaves for garnish	

❖ Peel and chop onion and fennel bulb. Reserve the feathery fennel tops for garnish.

Heat oil in a large Dutch oven. Add onion, fennel, garlic and carrot, and cook gently, making sure the garlic doesn't brown. Add peppers and continue cooking over low heat until they soften. Cool slightly. Purée mixture in a food processor.

Return mixture to the pan. Add tomato sauce and chicken stock. Heat and add salt and pepper, lemon juice and Galliano. Taste for seasoning. Serve at once, garnishing with sour cream and a wisp of fennel leaves. Serves 10 to 12.

COOK'S NOTE: This soup is even better if made the day before and reheated, but don't let it boil for hours or it will lose its kick. Add more Galliano at will.

If you can find a perfect pumpkin of an appropriate size, consider turning it into a tureen for the soup. Surround it with autumn leaves, sprigs of cedar and bunches of nuts or red berries.

BROCCOLI SALAD WITH SWEET YELLOW PEPPER

Vivid colors, crisp textures – a good foil for the softer, autumn dishes in this menu.

3 cups	broccoli florets	750 mL
1	yellow bell pepper	1
2 cups	cherry tomatoes, halved	500 mL
2	green onions, minced	2
1 3/4 cup	salad dressing	175 mL
1/4 cup	salad oil	50 mL
1 tbsp	dark soy sauce	15 mL
	salt and pepper	

❖   Be sure broccoli is cut into small, bite-size florets. Reserve stalk for another use. Cut bell pepper into thin strips.

Place broccoli, bell pepper, cherry tomato halves and onion in a salad bowl. Stir together salad dressing, salad oil and soy sauce. Pour over vegetables and toss well. Add salt and pepper to taste. Refrigerate salad at least 3 hours before serving. Serves 10 to 12.

On the Table

Thanksgiving is my favorite family feast of the entire year – it brings back all the warm colors, tastes and smells of harvest season. A basket of gourds, pomegranates and miniature pumpkins, surrounded by three bronze candles of varying heights, looks wonderful on either a bare wooden table with…

POTATOES WITH GARLIC CREAM GRATIN

These potatoes are a lusciously rich and creamy version of good old scalloped potatoes. Well-aged Asiago cheese may be used instead of Parmesan.

5 lb	baking potatoes	2.5 kg
3 tbsp	butter	30 mL
2 cups	cream	500 mL
2	cloves garlic, mashed	2
4 to 6 drops	Tabasco sauce	4 to 6 drops
	salt and pepper	
1/3 cup	Parmesan cheese, freshly grated	75 mL

❖ Peel potatoes but do not slice. Place in a bowl and cover with cold water. Set aside.

Butter a 9 x 13 inch (4 L) baking dish. Heat cream to boiling point. Stir in mashed garlic and Tabasco.

Pat potatoes dry. Slice as thin as possible, about 1/8 inch (3 mm) or less. Layer in the prepared dish. Lightly salt and pepper each layer. Pour hot garlic cream over potatoes. Sprinkle with cheese.

Bake 20 minutes in a 400 F (200 C) oven. Reduce heat to 350 F (180 C) and continue baking 40 minutes or until potatoes are tender. Let rest 10 minutes before serving. Serves 10 to 12.

COOK'S NOTE: This should be a creamy dish. Depending on the moisture content of your potatoes, they may require a drop more liquid. Check occasionally to see that they aren't drying out and add milk or cream as needed.

TURNIP CARROT CASSEROLE WITH PEARS

We always knew rutabagas as turnips and ignored the genuine turnip. Whatever you call them, they're even better done this way with carrots and pears.

1	19 oz (540 mL) can pear halves	1
1	large turnip (rutabaga)	1
4	large carrots	4
2	tbsp butter	30 mL
	salt and pepper	

❖ Drain pears, reserving juice for another use. Peel and dice turnip (rutabaga) and carrots. Cook in boiling water until tender. Drain. Put vegetables and pears in a food processor and purée. (They can be hand-mashed if you have the stamina.) Stir in butter, salt and pepper. Pour in a 6 cup (1.5 L) casserole. Serves 10 to 12.

COOK'S NOTE: I sometimes grate a wisp of nutmeg into this dish to enhance the flavor of the pears. The recipe can be made a day ahead and refrigerated.

…place mats or a cloth in any autumn shade: cinnamon, pumpkin, gold, forest green. If children are involved, show them how to make turkey place cards: on colored construction paper, trace their hand and extended fingers and thumb. The thumb becomes the head, the fingers make magnificent tail feathers.

WHITE CORN PUDDING WITH MOZZARELLA

The delicate kernels of the white corn steeped in butter have become a tradition at our house, and they're even better in this custardy presentation.

6	eggs	6
3 cups	white corn kernels	750 mL
1	green onion, minced	1
1 cup	mozzarella cheese, grated	250 mL
4 tbsp	flour	60 mL
1 tsp	sugar	5 mL
1 cup	milk	250 mL

salt and freshly ground pepper

❖ Preheat oven to 325 F (160 C).

In a large bowl, beat eggs thoroughly. Add corn, mixing well. Stir in remaining ingredients. (It will look like a thin soup, but don't worry).

Pour into a buttered 1 1/2 quart (1.5 L) casserole. Bake 1 hour and 20 minutes or until puffed and golden. (A knife inserted in the center should come out clean.) Serve hot.

Serves 10 to 12.

SPICED CRANBERRY APPLE COMPOTE

Cranberries and turkey are an unbeatable combination, but just for a change, try cranberries, apple and ginger with turkey.

1 cup	water	250 mL
2/3 cup	sugar	150 mL
3 tsp	candied ginger, slivered	15 mL
1/2 tsp	cinnamon	2 mL
1	apple, diced	1
2 cups	whole cranberries	500 mL

❖ Put water, sugar and candied ginger in a saucepan. Bring to a boil and cook until sugar dissolves. Add cinnamon, diced apple and cranberries. Reduce heat and simmer without stirring until berries pop and sauce thickens. Remove from heat and cool. Serve with turkey. Makes about 2 cups (500 mL).

TURKEY WITH EGG BREAD STUFFING

Whether I buy a frozen turkey, or have the occasional luxury of a fresh wild turkey from a local grower, egg bread makes the best stuffing. I buy my turkeys with a pound of meat per person in mind, especially if it's a wild bird, which has a bit more bone-to-meat than domestic birds. That way I end up with a generously filled platter, and there are always a few toothsome leftovers.

12 lb	turkey	5.5 kg
	salt and pepper	

STUFFING

1/2 cup	butter	125 mL
1	large onion, chopped	1
2 cups	white mushrooms, diced	500 mL
3 stalks	celery, with leaves, chopped	3
1	apple, diced	1
1 tsp	salt	5 mL
4 tsp	thyme	20 mL
1 tsp	tarragon	5 mL
1/2 cup	fresh parsley, minced	125 mL
1 tsp	black pepper	5 mL
12 cups	cubed egg bread	3 L
2 tsp	instant chicken granules	10 mL
1 cup	hot water	250 mL

❖ Wipe turkey with a damp cloth, making sure that all odd bits and excess fat have been removed. Sprinkle cavity lightly with salt and pepper.

Make stuffing. In a large saucepan, melt butter. Cook vegetables with apple, salt and herbs over medium heat, until soft but not browned.

Put bread cubes in a large mixing bowl. Pour cooked vegetables and their juices over the top and toss.

Dissolve chicken granules in hot water. Drizzle over stuffing and toss again.

Fill cavity of bird loosely with stuffing. Fill neck cavity. Carefully separate the skin of the breast from the meat and lightly stuff. (Too much stuffing here will result in burst skin.)

Truss turkey and place in a roaster, breast up. Cover with foil and roast at 325 F (160 C) roughly 4 hours, basting bird with pan juices.

During the last hour of roasting, remove foil to encourage browning. Turkey is done when a meat thermometer in the thigh registers 185 F (85 C). Let turkey cool, covered, about 15 minutes before carving so juices will have a chance to set.

Serves 12, with leftovers.

In the Bottle

The gentle flavors are an ideal chance to showcase wine, and roast bird is a fine foil to any delicate red, so this is the time to drink old wine. Pull out the aged vintage cabernets or a fine old pinot noir you've been saving. If you prefer something younger, go for a particularly rich and buttery chardonnay. Most premium Californians will fill the bill. French white burgundy is good too, and this isn't a bad meal to try your old German Rieslings. For a crowd, add a couple of bottles of chenin blanc, chardonnay, merlot and fresh young Chianti.

STEAMED CRANBERRY PUDDING WITH ORANGE CUSTARD SAUCE

Steamed puddings remind me of home, especially in the autumn. This old Nova Scotia pud, made with juicy bog-grown berries, rather than the smaller high-bush berries, has a tart-sweet flavor that is sharpened with orange juice and mellowed with orange custard sauce. Along with steamed carrot pudding, it's one of my favorite desserts in autumn or winter.

1/2 cup	butter	125 mL
3/4 cup	granulated sugar	175 mL
2	eggs	2
1/2 cup	orange juice	125 mL
1 tsp	orange rind, grated	5 mL
2 1/3 cups	flour	575 mL
3 tsp	baking powder	15 mL
1/2 tsp	salt	2 mL
2 cups	whole cranberries	500 mL

❖ Cream butter and sugar until light and fluffy. Beat in eggs, orange juice and rind. Sift together flour, baking powder and salt, and add to butter mixture, alternating with milk. Fold in cranberries.

Butter and flour a 6 cup (1.5 L) pudding mold. The batter will be quite thick, so spoon it in and pack well. Cover with a lid or a double thickness of tin foil buttered and secured with an elastic band.

Put the mold in a larger cooking pot (roaster or Dutch oven) and add boiling water until it reaches halfway up the mold. Bring the water to a boil and immediately lower heat to simmer. Cover. Steam 2 hours, adding more water if necessary. Let pudding rest 15 minutes before unmolding. Serves 8.

COOK'S NOTE: This pudding may be cooled to room temperature and frozen up to 2 months. To reheat, thaw and steam or microwave until hot through.

ORANGE CUSTARD SAUCE

I used to serve a cranberry custard sauce with the cranberry pudding, but the orange sauce plays up the hint of orange in the pudding and is, I think, a more successful partner.

1 cup	milk	250 mL
1/4 cup	granulated sugar	50 mL
1/2 tsp	orange rind, grated	2 mL
	pinch salt	
3	egg yolks	3
	juice of 1 orange	
1 tbsp	orange marmalade	15 mL
1/2 cup	whipping cream, whipped	125 mL

❖ Scald milk. Stir in sugar, orange rind and salt.

In the top of a double boiler, beat egg yolks and gradually stir in milk. Cook over simmering water, beating with a wire whisk until custard thickens slightly and will coat a spoon. Cool custard, placing a circle of wax paper directly on the surface to keep a skin from forming.

Stir in orange juice and marmalade. Cover closely and refrigerate.

To serve, fold in whipped cream and pour sauce in an open bowl that has a serving ladle, as the sauce spoons better than it pours. Makes nearly 3 cups (750 mL).

PUMPKIN FLAN WITH MAPLE CREAM

This is like a good pumpkin pie without the crust. Make it in a ring mold and garnish the top (or slather it completely) with whipped cream. Be sure you use freshly grated nutmeg – just buy the smallest bag of whole nutmegs you can find and grate them yourself. The pulverized stuff that's been sitting for months in a tin can isn't a patch on the flavor of fresh nutmeg.

2	eggs	2
14 oz	can pumpkin	398 mL
3/4 cup	brown sugar, packed	175 mL
1 tbsp	dark molasses	15 mL
2 tbsp	cinnamon	10 mL
1 tsp	ginger	5 mL
1/2 tsp	nutmeg, freshly grated	2 mL
1/2 tsp	salt	2 mL
1 1/4 cups	evaporated milk	300 mL

❖ Preheat oven to 425 F (220 C).

In a large bowl, beat together eggs, pumpkin, sugar, molasses, spices and salt. Beat in evaporated milk.

Butter a 4 cup (1 L) tube pan and pour in pumpkin mixture. Place the tube pan in a larger pan. Once in the oven, pour boiling water in the outer pan halfway up the mold.

Bake 10 minutes at 425 F (220 C). Reduce heat to 325 F (160 C) and continue baking about 45 minutes or until a knife inserted in the pumpkin comes out clean.

Let cool in pan. Run a knife around the edge and carefully invert onto a large serving plate. May be garnished with whipped cream, but as a special treat try Maple Cream. Serves 10.

MAPLE CREAM

1 cup	whipping cream	250 mL
1/2 tsp	maple flavoring	2 mL
1/4 cup	maple syrup	50 mL

❖ Whip cream until soft peaks form. Stir in maple flavoring and syrup. Continue whipping until it reaches the desired stiffness.

APRICOT NUT BROWNIES

A chewy option to dark chocolate brownies, these golden brownies play up the intense flavor of dried apricots and almonds. I used to ice them with white chocolate or brown sugar icing, but a light dusting of icing sugar is really enough.

4 oz	white chocolate	125 g
1/3 cup	butter	75 mL
1/2 cup	sugar	125 mL
2	eggs	2
1/4 tsp	almond extract	1 mL
3/4 cup	all-purpose flour	175 mL
1/2 tsp	baking powder	2 mL
1/4 tsp	salt	1 mL
1 cup	dried apricots, finely chopped	250 mL
1/2 cup	slivered almonds	125 mL

❖ Adjust oven rack to the middle position and preheat oven to 350 F (180 C). Grease a 9 inch (2.5 L) cake pan.

In a large saucepan, combine white chocolate and butter. Melt over low heat until mixture begins to curdle. Remove from heat. Add sugar, eggs and extract, and stir quickly to blend.

In a separate bowl, combine flour, baking powder and salt. Stir flour mixture into white chocolate mixture. Add half the dried apricots and almonds. Stir to blend.

Pour in the prepared pan. Sprinkle the top with remaining apricots and almonds. Bake 25 to 30 minutes or until golden and brownies begin to pull away from the edge of the pan.

Remove from oven and cool in the pan placed on wire rack.

When cool, dust with icing sugar and cut into about 30 pieces.

THE AFTERMATH

Every Thanksgiving I read a number of instructive pieces about the economics of making a single turkey last through the next week. Personally, I think three days is all one can reasonably ask of the average bird.

I like it roasted on The Day and cold the day after, with lots of warmed-up vegetables and the last dab of cranberries. Then I like a few extra slices in a sandwich before bed.

On the third day I consign the remains – skin, bones and whatever else is left – to the soup pot.

Turkey soup will look after all the odds and ends that the cook is sick of looking at and doesn't know what to do with. It also will take care of the neck, the rib cage, and whatever limp vegetables might be lying about. Celery leaves are wonderful, as are carrots, which should be scrubbed but not peeled.

You'll need a bay leaf, an onion, a bunch of parsley and a clove of garlic. Put everything in a big soup pot or Dutch oven, cover with cold water and simmer about four hours or until it smells maddeningly delicious.

Pour through a colander, saving only the liquid. Chill the soup stock thoroughly so you can lift off the fat.

To finish the soup, bring the stock to a boil with whatever vegetables you wish – I like to chop in an onion, a stalk of celery, a carrot for sweetness and a slice of turnip for zest. If you have leftover turkey meat, chuck it in the pot too. Add a handful of short grain rice and simmer everything together for 30 minutes or until the rice and vegetables are tender. Taste the soup and correct the seasonings; it may need extra salt or a pinch of thyme.

Now ladle it into broad soup plates with a smash of freshly chopped parsley over top, eat it with crusty bread and butter, and finish off with a baked apple or some equally simple, homey dessert like Fast Track Punkin'.

That's it. Soup for everybody. With luck, you won't see another turkey until Christmas.

FAST TRACK PUNKIN'

No time for the real thing? This is amazingly good made with canned pumpkin pie filling – not to be confused with plain canned pumpkin.

1 cup	half-and-half	250 mL
2 cups	seasoned pumpkin pie filling	500 mL
1	pkg instant vanilla pudding	1
1 cup	whipped cream	250 mL

❖ Beat together half-and-half, seasoned pie filling and vanilla pudding mix. Taste for seasoning. (You may wish for a dash more cinnamon or a fast pass with the nutmeg grater.) Pour pumpkin mixture in a pretty, 4 cup (1 L) dish. Garnish with whipped cream. Chill about 1 hour. Serve from the dish. Serves 8.

A Celebration of New Wine

There will be a Sunday sometime between now and Christmas when you feel like cooking something warm and solid, drawing a cork or two and sharing it all with friends. If the day happens to fall near November 15, you could make a party of it, and celebrate the arrival of the nouveau Beaujolais.

The annual unveiling of the new wine in Beaujolais causes such fuss that political coups and the juiciest scandals pale by comparison. All over the civilized world, otherwise sensible, sane wine lovers go a bit balmy in the rush to be first at the jug.

A few years ago, the nouveau Beaujolais threatened to become so popular that there was scarcely enough left for the locals, who naturally felt they had first dibs. Rumblings were heard in other wine regions.

Enter the Italians, who noticed that the French were having phenomenal success selling good but ordinary red wines that were still too young to drink.

Smelling money, they came up with their own version of Beaujolais nouveau and called it vino novello. The fizzy new Italian wine won instant fans, especially among wine lovers who objected to the skyrocketing price of Beaujolais.

Before long, a whole flock of nouveau/novello/primeur wines had been hatched, all riding on the coattails of the wildly successful French. In a northern Alberta town called Grande Prairie, a small winery specializing in native fruit wines came up with

Three Cheese Puff Pastry

Spicy Pâté

---

*Cajun Beans with Rice and
Hot Sausage*

---

*Mimi's Pear Flan with
Buttery Almond Crust*

---

*Platter with Fruit, Nuts
and Cheese
(see* On the Table
for suggestions)

something called Saskatoon nouveau (after the little, blue berry of the same name). *Alors, mes enfants!* It sold out as fast as they could bottle it.

Though Saskatoon nouveau made no waves in France, vino novello did not escape notice. The French, never given to modesty in the matter of wine making, were not amused by the pretentious little upstart from the south. Its annual appearance on the heels of the Beaujolais nouveau is greeted with predictable snarls by loyal Frenchmen everywhere.

Most of the genuine Beaujolais arriving for the November fête is produced by honorable men who have earned respectability in the wine world, and what they ship is drinkable. But the cachet of the thing is associated as much with the race as the wine itself. If it can be transhipped via motorbike, water ski, jeep, mule train and eventually dropped by parachute from a World War I Sopwith Camel, the local paparazzi will be out in force, which is what this is really about.

The infant wine, snatched too early from its cellar, seldom improves during its frenetic travels and often seems to be suffering from shock. Still, it makes for a good party.

The celebrants drink it fast, with none of the usual slurping, snuffling and spitting that accompanies more serious tastings. The vocabulary of wine, fodder for some of the world's most pretentious bores, takes an earthier turn. Benjie and Muffie, freed of having to blather on about acacia-after-rain, ripe mulberries and other things they've never smelled, speak from their hearts.

"Twigs, Muffie. I taste twigs."

Muffie plunges her nose into the glass before announcing triumphantly, "No, Benjie, I'm getting leaves. Dead leaves. And grass clippings. Old grass clippings."

And so, having declared the pride of Beaujolais to be just this side of compost, they toss back another glass and fall joyfully upon the pâté.

Which is exactly the way it should unfold. Beaujolais is a joyous wine, one to drink young and slightly cool, with solid, gutsy food, lots of laughing and maybe some kind of interesting trouble before the night is over.

The respected American wine writer, Kermit Lynch, described Beaujolais as rude and flirtatious, the one-night stand of wine. Nobody could have said it better.

This menu is perfect for a long, lazy afternoon tasting that lingers into evening. Serve the cheese and the pâté early, and offer the beans and rice later, when the party needs refuelling.

THREE CHEESE PUFF PASTRY

This delicious pastry is similar to *le gatis*, a dish from the Southwest of France that uses brioche instead of puff pastry. Almost any cheese may be used, including (for a special treat) part Stilton, Roquefort or Gorgonzola.

I buy puff pastry in 14.5 oz (411 g) packages and use only half that amount in this recipe. The rest of the pastry must remain frozen. (If it thaws in the fridge, use it within two days.)

1/2	14.5 oz (411 g) pkg puff pastry dough	1/2
1	small Camembert	1
6 oz	old Cheddar cheese	185 g
5 oz	goat cheese	155 g
1	egg	1
	freshly ground pepper	
	egg wash: 1 egg beaten with 1 tbsp (15 mL) milk	

❖ Preheat over to 425 F (220 C).

Divide the puff pastry in half. Roll out each piece on a lightly floured board into about a 10 inch (25 cm) circle. Refrigerate until ready to use.

Cut all cheese into chunks, but do not remove rind from Camembert. Place in a food processor with egg and pepper, and pulse until it almost forms a mass.

Remove dough from refrigerator. Working with a rubber spatula, mound cheese evenly over one circle of the dough, leaving a 1 inch (2.5 cm) border all around.

Brush the border with egg wash. Place the second puff pastry circle over the first. Press and roll the edges together. Make four small slashes in the top crust. Brush crust with egg wash. Place on a baking sheet and bake about 20 minutes or until the tart is puffed and golden brown. Serve barely warm or at room temperature.

Serves 6 as a light entrée or 10 as an appetizer.

On the Table

Use the dessert as decoration. Go shopping in the Italian district for fresh figs. Also, buy small pears, two or three varieties of grapes, some small shiny tangerines and Granny Smith apples. On a rough wooden board, arrange the fruit with a bowl of walnuts in their shells and a wheel of good Camembert or a selection of favorite cheeses. Don't forget the pear flan. An arrangement of tall black or deep red candles in brass holders just behind the food has a dramatic effect. Use three, five or seven candles of varying heights.

SPICY PÂTÉ

There's a hint of curry in this soft buttery pâté, but it's so subtle that instead of interfering with the wine, it only enhances the pleasure. The delicate mousselike texture and luxuriously rich ingredients make it one of my favorite things to serve with a variety of breads and interesting crackers. Note: There are three additions of butter. This is not a dish for weight worriers.

2 cups	onion, chopped	500 mL
1/4 cup	butter	50 mL
1 lb	chicken livers	500 g
1/4 cup	butter	50 mL
1/2 cup	whipping cream	125 mL
1/4 cup	cognac	50 mL
2 tbsp	port	30 mL
2	garlic cloves, minced	2
1 tsp	thyme	5 mL
1 tsp	curry powder	5 mL
1 1/2 tsp	salt	7 mL
1/4 cup	fresh parsley, coarsely chopped	50 mL
1/2 cup	butter	125 mL
	salt and pepper	

❖ In a large frying pan, sauté onions in butter until just transparent.

Trim chicken livers and cut into small pieces. Melt second addition of butter in the same pan with onions and fry chicken livers. Let cool.

In a food processor place onions, livers and juices. Add cream, cognac and port. Pulse on and off until puréed. Add garlic, thyme, curry powder, salt and parsley.

Put third addition of butter in the machine and pulse until blended and quite fluffy in texture. Taste for seasoning, adding more salt if necessary.

Scoop mixture into a crock or bowl, or mound on a plate. Surround the base with roughly chopped parsley. Serve with a variety of breads and raw vegetables such as carrot sticks, celery sticks, red and yellow sweet bell peppers.

May be refrigerated up to 4 days or frozen for 2 months. Makes about 2 cups (500 mL).

CAJUN BEANS WITH RICE AND HOT SAUSAGE

The soft pulpy beans marry well with the spicy sausage and salty ham.

1	19 oz (540 mL) can white kidney beans, undrained	1
1	19 oz (540 mL) can red kidney beans, undrained	1
2 cups	diced ham	500 mL
12	fresh Cajun sausages	12
1	large onion, diced	1
1	large celery stalk, with leaves, diced	1
1	green pepper, diced	1
4	green onions, including tops, sliced	4
2	cloves garlic, minced	2
1/2 cup	fresh parsley, minced	125 mL
2	large bay leaves	2
2 tsp	thyme, crumbled	10 mL
2 tsp	oregano, crumbled	10 mL
	salt and pepper	
	Tabasco sauce	
2 cups	long-grain rice	500 mL
	diced tomato and minced green onion for garnish	

continues…

❖ Preheat broiler.

Prick sausage all over and broil until browned, turning once. Carefully pour juices from sausages in a Dutch oven and reserve. Let sausage cool, then slice into bite-sized chunks and reserve.

To reserved sausage juices, add ham, onion, celery, green pepper and green onions. Fry over medium heat until onion is transparent. Add garlic and fry 1 minute longer. Stir in beans and their liquid, reserved sausage and seasonings.

Add water to cover bean mixture by about 1 inch (2.5 cm). Bring to simmer. Cook, uncovered, stirring occasionally, about 1 hour or until a thick sauce has formed.

Meanwhile, cook rice as directed.

To serve, mound rice on a large deep platter, leaving lots of room around the edge. Ladle bean mixture all around rice. Remove bay leaf before serving. Sprinkle beans with diced tomato and rice with minced green onion. Serve immediately. Serves 10 to 12 as a side dish or 6 as a main course.

MIMI'S PEAR FLAN WITH BUTTERY ALMOND CRUST

Nobody seems to know who Mimi was, but I'll say this for her – the girl could cook. Mimi's flan is full of voluptuous flavors and seductive aromas, perfect for an evening of sassy young wines.

Some people make the crust in a food processor, but I find that a pastry blender works best. Anjou pears have a good texture for this pie, as long as they're fully ripe and of uniform size. Do use a flan ring for the best presentation of this scrumptious dessert.

CRUST

3/4 cup	flour	175 mL
1/4 cup	ground almonds	50 mL
3 tbsp	sugar	45 mL
1/2 cup	cold butter	125 mL
1/2 tsp	almond extract	2 mL
1	egg, beaten	1

❖ Put flour, almonds and sugar in a medium bowl. Cut in butter with a pastry blender.

Stir almond extract into beaten egg and add to flour mixture, stirring with a fork only until it forms a ball. Place dough in the middle of a 9 inch (23 cm) flan ring with removable rim and gently pat and push crust into shape, bringing it up the edge. Chill crust at least 30 minutes before baking.

FILLING

5	pears	5
1/2 cup	butter	125 mL
2/3 cup	sugar	150 mL
1 cup	ground almonds	250 mL
3	eggs	3
2 tsp	vanilla	10 mL
1 tsp	almond extract	5 mL
1/2 cup	sliced almonds	125 mL
	icing sugar	

❖ Preheat oven to 375 F (190 C).

Peel, core and halve pears. Drop into water to which you've added a splash of white vinegar or lemon juice. (This will keep the pears from discoloring.)

Be sure butter isn't ice-cold. Beat together butter, sugar, ground almonds, eggs, vanilla and almond extract. Pour in the pie shell. Drain pear halves and pat dry. Place 9 pear halves (or 7, if pears are large) in a circle with stem-end pointing inward. Place remaining half in center. Bake 20 minutes.

Reduce heat to 325 F (160 C) and bake 15 minutes more. Strew sliced almonds over flan and continue baking about 25 to 30 minutes. Let cool about 15 minutes. Dust with icing sugar. Serves 8 to 10.

In the Bottle

Vino novello is cheaper than Beaujolais nouveau, and most people can't tell the difference. But there's so much new wine coming on the market during this season, even new Muscadet, so aim for the widest possible selection and taste them back and forth.

The Royal Pears

One Christmas, when I was ten and grandma was eighty-something, I watched the night train drop the usual sacks of potatoes and mail at our railway station house and roar away into the east, toward the bright lights of Clair and Wadena. Shortly afterward, Grandma and I were summoned to the freight shed.

A dim, chilly den with deep shelves along both sides, the shed had its own smell, a heady blend of all the things it held: onions and cabbages, rubber tires, apples, baby chicks. For me it was a cross between Eaton's and heaven.

On that particular evening my father pointed to a big cardboard box with two names on it – Grandma's and mine.

In the upper corner were the words Harry and David's Royal Riviera Pears and a picture of two men. They looked thirtyish and healthy in their plaid shirts, and I could see by their smiles that Harry and David had a good dentist.

The box was lined with a cloud of soft, silvery stuff, and nestled within were two dozen pears, each individually wrapped in purple foil.

Grandma picked one up. "My, my!" she said. (Grandma said that a lot. You just had to know what mood she was in to figure out which "My, my" she meant). She turned the pear round and round in her hand. "Royal purple pears," she said in a thoughtful

A Christmas Eve Supper

———

Christmas Potpie

———

Stuffed Country Ham

———

Big Green Salad

———

Dill Bread with Cheese

———

Chutney Baked Pears

———

Sweet Molasses Mustard

———

*Carrot Pudding with
Two Sauces*

———

Bûche de Nöel

———

White Chocolate Cheesecake

way, but when she unwrapped it, that pear was perfectly golden.

Harry and David had enclosed a nice card inviting Grandma and me to join the Fruit of the Month Club and informing us that the royal pears had been paid for by the California aunt. At the time I had a variety of aunts – some were ordinary, a few were devoutly religious, but the California aunt was a true exotic. She'd been married three times and had her own grapefruit tree.

The only husband I'd met was the third and present, who had accompanied her on a visit the previous summer.

With my little brother, Bud, I had ample opportunity to study him at close range. He was bigger and louder than anyone had a right to be. He had a passion for oversized cars and plaid shirts, which he felt were essential when traveling in Canada. And he had a habit of grabbing the nearest female relative and clutching her to his broad, plaid chest, bellowing, "Gimme a hug, sweet thing!" (He pronounced it "thang".)

My father, a reserved man not given to bear-hugging distant female relatives, was not impressed. Nor was Grandma. During the many years they shared the same table and the same roof, it was the only time I remember Grandma and Dad agreeing on anything.

The new uncle seemed to know a lot about food. In fact it was his favorite subject, and when he said he had a present for me, I expected candy or at least a grapefruit from my aunt's tree. Imagine my surprise when he dived into the trunk of his car and came up with a tiny jar of pickled artichoke hearts. I thanked him, and Bud and I listened while he lectured us about artichokes in the Salad Bowl of Civilization, which is what he called the Salinas Valley, where he and the California aunt lived.

I tried to trade my artichokes for Bud's water pistol, but he wasn't interested. Then I tried to give them to Grandma, but she said it was a sin to give away a gift, so I knew she didn't want them either. Every now and then I'd shake the jar and watch my artichokes roll around, but as presents went, they ranked right up there with winter undershirts.

One day, the new uncle made pancakes. The minute he announced his intention, I smelled trouble. Bud and I were in the backyard helping him admire his car when he made one of his periodic dives into the trunk and came up with a bag of buckwheat flour. "I'm gonna make you kids a batch of the world's best pancakes," he yelled, shattering the calm of a Saskatchewan morning. My dog started to bark.

I considered telling him that Dad already made the world's best pancakes about once a month or so and that he might not be thrilled to learn that his only competition had married into the family, but it didn't seem like a thing the new uncle would want to hear, so I kept quiet.

The pancakes took a long time. There was a lot of commotion in the kitchen, with spilled milk and buckwheat dust everywhere and a lot of giggling while the California aunt tied one of Grandma's aprons around his considerable girth and got bear-hugged nearly to death.

When the new contenders for the world's best pancakes were finally loaded aboard my mother's Sunday platter, they were stunningly ordinary, in a dry sort of way. They weren't in the same league with the ones we were accustomed to eating.

My mother declared them "interesting." Grandma said, "My, my!" Dad smiled, and after that he referred to the new uncle as "That Windbag Your Aunt Married."

My aunt, who was a wise woman in spite of a weakness for the wrong men, watched the whole performance, saying nothing, but understanding everything. So when the royal pears arrived at Christmas, Grandma and I decided that was the reason. Because of the pancakes and probably the bear hugs.

They were terrific pears. Wonderful pears. Crisply, sweetly, juicily delicious within their purple wrappers, with none of the gritty bits I hated in those lesser pears we canned every year.

As Christmas drew nearer, Grandma and I ran our own Fruit of the Month Club. After school I'd run upstairs to her room over the railway tracks, and we'd split a royal pear while the juice dripped off our chins and I read to her from the Personals, our favorite column in the Family Herald.

"Ukrainian Farmer , Garden, Cow, seek Houskpr. Marriage if suited. Send pic."

Grandma would say, "My, my!" and laugh so hard her eyes would get tears in them. I'd laugh and fall off the chair, and my dog would bark, and we'd split another pear.

All these years later, I still find Harry and David grinning at me from the December pages of Gourmet Magazine, the picture of eternal youth with their plaid shirts and shiny teeth, and I remember Grandma and the royal Christmas pears.

Having covered the turkey tradition in October, my December menu works well on the other days of celebration - Christmas Eve, or Boxing Day, or even New Year's Day, if you're up to cooking. All of it except the salad can be prepared well ahead of time; cook's deserve a Christmas break, too.

CHRISTMAS POTPIE

On Christmas Eve after midnight mass, my cousin Michelline serves a French Canadian *reveillon* with traditional *tourtiere*. My potpie isn't *tourtiere*, but it's something close, and it's a good dish to serve if you're having a crowd.

Serve the potpie or the ham. If you're having a big crowd, say 20 or more, do both.

1 lb	beef steak	500 g
2 lbs	pork tenderloin	1 kg
1 tbsp	oil	15 mL
1	clove garlic, mashed	1
1	large onion, diced	1
1	carrot, diced	1
1 cup	turnip, diced	250 mL
1	stalk celery, diced	1
1 tsp	cinnamon	5 mL
1 tsp	sage	5 mL
1/4 cup	ketchup	50 mL
1 cup	beef stock	250 mL
	salt and pepper	
	puff pastry for 9 inch (23 cm) pie	

❖ Freeze meat slightly so it will be easy to slice. Cut meat into fine dice. Heat oil in a Dutch oven and brown meat, working in batches. Remove and reserve meat.

Add garlic and vegetables to the pan, and stir-fry briefly. Add seasonings and ketchup. Cover and cook about 5 minutes over medium heat.

Add meat and beef stock. Cook, covered, over low heat about 1 hour. Uncover, increase heat and cook about 15 minutes to reduce juices. (The mixture should be moist but not runny.) Add salt and pepper.

Remove from heat and cool completely. The mixture may be refrigerated overnight or frozen.

Scoop mixture into a 2 qt (2 L) casserole. Brush the rim of the dish with water, and cover with rolled puff pastry, pressing it onto the edge to seal well. Scallop or crimp the crust, and decorate the top with pastry leaves or other artistic squiggles. Refrigerate until ready to bake.

About 50 minutes before serving, cut slits in crust and brush with egg wash made by beating together 1 egg yolk and 2 tbsp (30 mL) of water. Bake at 450 F (230 C) for 12 minutes. Reduce heat to 350 F (180 C) and continue baking 30 minutes longer, until crust is golden brown. Pie also may be frozen, then baked at 425 F (220 C) for 1 hour. Serves 10 to 12.

STUFFED COUNTRY HAM

Baked ham, stuffed with spicy sausage meat laced with mincemeat, is about as festive as a party meat can ever be. This superb buffet ham, with its side dish of stuffing, has been adapted from a recipe by the Canadian Home Economics Association and Five Roses Flour. It's just as festive at Easter or New Years as it is at Christmas.

8 to 10 lb	ham, boned and cooked	3.5 to 4 .5 kg
	curly kale or endive for garnish	

STUFFING

3 lbs	pork sausage	1.5 kg
1/4 cup	butter	50 mL
1 cup	celery, chopped	250 mL
1 cup	onion, chopped	250 mL
1	apple, diced	1
1 cup	mincemeat	250 mL
1 cup	oatmeal	250 mL
2 tsp	thyme	10 mL
1 1/2 cups	corn chips, crushed	375 mL
1 1/2 cups	bread crumbs	375 mL
1/2 cup	fresh parsley, chopped	125 mL

continues…

GLAZE

1/2 cup	honey	125 mL
3 tbsp	Dijon mustard	50 mL

❖ Brown sausage meat in a large Dutch oven. Break up with a fork and add butter, celery, onion and apple. Cook until onion is transparent. Add mincemeat, oatmeal, thyme, corn chips and bread crumbs. Toss lightly. Add parsley and toss again until thoroughly mixed. Allow stuffing to cool.

Cut 6 lengthwise slits in ham, 5 inches (12 cm) deep and 1/2 inch (1 cm) apart. Spoon stuffing into the slits but do not pack. Put remaining stuffing in a buttered casserole and reserve.

Bake stuffed ham at 325 F (160 C) about 1 1/2 hours.

Mix glaze and brush liberally over ham. Return ham to oven with extra stuffing. Bake about 30 minutes longer.

Let ham stand at least 30 minutes before slicing or serve it cold. Garnish with curly kale or endive. Serves 12, with leftovers.

BIG GREEN SALAD

An easy salad to throw together, the Big Green has enough acid and bite to balance the richer dishes in this meal. Serve in a huge glass bowl if possible.

5	seedless oranges, peeled and sliced	5
1	red onion, sliced	1
2	large romaine heads	2
1 cup	croutons	250 mL
1/2 cup	salad oil	125 mL
1/3 cup	olive oil	75 mL
2 tsp	orange rind, grated	10 mL
	juice of 1 orange	
4 tbsp	vinegar	60 mL
1	clove garlic, mashed	1
	dash of Tabasco sauce	
	salt and pepper	

❖ Tear washed romaine into bite-size pieces. Add orange slices and onion rings. Have croutons ready.

Combine remaining ingredients in a jar and shake briskly. Pour over salad ingredients, and toss. Sprinkle with croutons and toss again. Serves 12.

DILL BREAD WITH CHEESE

This fragrant bread has a moist coarse texture because of the cheese, and it is delicious fresh. It makes wonderful toast the second day. I often make it in a food processor to speed things up.

1	pkg active dry yeast	1
2 tbsp	sugar	30 mL
1/4 cup	lukewarm water (105 to 115 F)	50 mL
1 cup	creamed cottage cheese	250 mL
1 tsp	dry mustard	5 mL
1 tsp	mustard seeds	5 mL
1 tbsp	dillweed	15 mL
1 tbsp	butter, melted	15 mL
1/4 tsp	baking soda	1 mL
1	egg, beaten	1
2 1/4 to 2 1/2 cups	all-purpose flour	550 to 625 mL
	melted butter and coarse salt for the top of the baked loaf	

❖ In the bowl of a food processor, sprinkle yeast and sugar over warm water. Pulse once. Leave 10 minutes.

Heat cottage cheese just enough to take off the chill. (It must not be hot or cold.) Add cheese, mustards, dillweed and butter to yeast mixture, and pulse just until cheese is smooth. Add baking soda and egg. Pulse once.

Add most of the flour and process until dough cleans the bowl. Add remaining flour if necessary.

Lightly oil a 1 1/2 qt (1.5 L) casserole and turn the dough into it. Cover and set aside to rise in a draft-free place until double in size, about 1 hour.

Preheat oven to 350 F (180 C).

Bake bread in the center of the oven for 40 to 50 minutes, until it is lightly browned on top and the bottom sounds hollow when tapped. Brush top of loaf with melted butter and sprinkle with coarse salt while still hot. Let cool before slicing. For a buffet, serve on a decorative bread board with a sharp knife so guests can cut their own. Makes 1 loaf.

CHUTNEY BAKED PEARS

Use a firm winter pear that can stand up to the baking – preferably Anjou. Although you can substitute almost any good chutney, including pear, Major Grey has a special flavor that is wonderful in this dish.

6	winter pears	
2 cups	Major Grey chutney	500 mL
6 tsp	butter	30 mL

❖ Peel, core and halve the pears. To prevent discoloration, drop pears into acidulated water made by combining 2 tbsp (30 mL) lemon juice or white vinegar per quart (L) of water.

Pour chutney in a blender and chop coarsely, using on-off bursts.

Butter a large baking dish that can go to the table, about 9 x 13 inches (4 L). Arrange pears snugly in the pan, cored-side up. Distribute chutney evenly among pears. Top with butter. Bake 30 minutes at 350 F (180 C). Serves 12.

SWEET MOLASSES MUSTARD

A dark, sweet mustard that gets an extra punch from the molasses, this mustard goes especially well with the stuffed ham.

1/4 cup	cider vinegar	50 mL
1/4 cup	honey	50 mL
2 tbsp	molasses	30 mL
1 tsp	vegetable oil	5 mL
1/4 cup	dry mustard	50 mL
1 tbsp	mustard seeds	15 mL
1 tsp	all-purpose flour	5 mL
1/4 tsp	salt	1 mL

❖ Put vinegar, honey, molasses, brown sugar and oil in a small saucepan and simmer about 5 minutes, stirring constantly so it doesn't stick or scorch. Remove from heat and stir in dry mustard, mustard seed and flour. Return to heat and cook, whisking constantly, until it begins to bubble and thickens slightly. Stir in salt. Pour in a jar and let cool before sealing with a tight-fitting lid. Refrigerate 24 hours before serving to allow flavors to mellow. Makes about 3/4 cup (175 mL).

In the Bottle

A Beaujolais Grand Cru from the current vintage, particularly a Regnié, the newest area to be designated a grand cru, is a fine choice with the ham. You don't want something heavyweight like Morgon or Moulin-a-Vent. A Fleurie, Julienas, Chiroubles or Saint-Amour, particularly from a good house like Georges Duboeuf, is a perfect match. The Beaujolais goes well with the baked pears too. If you want a white, go for a chenin blanc or a full-flavored and mildly sweet Riesling.

BUCHE DE NÖEL

There are quick-and-dirty Yule logs made with instant puddings, and ice cream Yule logs from your friendly frozen foodmonger, but this coffee-flavored cake with its rich but light filling is the ultimate *bûche de nöel* from a wonderful Quebecois cook.

I always plant a tall red candle in the middle and keep it lit while serving slices from either end.

CAKE

5	eggs	5
1 cup	granulated sugar	250 mL
1 1/4 cups	cake flour	300 mL
1 tsp	baking powder	5 mL
1/2 tsp	baking soda	2 mL
1 tbsp	instant coffee granules	15 mL

❖ Preheat oven to 400 F (200 C).

Line an 11 x 17 inch (28 x 43 cm) jelly roll pan with buttered and floured foil.

Beat eggs until frothy, then beat in sugar.

Sift and measure flour. Stir in baking powder, baking soda and coffee granules. Fold flour mixture into egg mixture. Pour in the prepared pan and bake in the oven 10 to 15 minutes or until top springs back when lightly touched.

Turn out on a tea towel that has been sprinkled with icing sugar. Roll cake lengthwise in the towel and set aside for 10 minutes. Unroll while still slightly warm so it doesn't break. Cool.

FILLING

1 tsp	unflavored gelatin	5 mL
1 tbsp	water	15 mL
1 cup	whipping cream	250 mL
3 tbsp	brown sugar	45 mL
1 tbsp	instant coffee granules	15 mL

❖ Sprinkle gelatin over water and let stand for a few minutes to soften. Heat in microwave or over hot water to dissolve gelatin, then let cool to room temperature. Whip cream until stiff peaks form. Fold in gelatin, brown sugar and coffee granules. Spread over cooled cake and reroll, starting at long end.

MOCHA BUTTER ICING

1/4 cup	soft butter	50 mL
2 cups	icing sugar, sifted	500 mL
1/3 cup	cocoa	75 mL
1/2 tsp	ground cloves	2 mL
2 tbsp	instant coffee	30 mL
1/4 cup	cream	50 mL

❖ Cream butter. Add icing sugar, cocoa, cloves, coffee granules and cream. Beat until thick and fluffy. Put filled cake on a serving board or platter. Cut a small diagonal slice off one end of cake and place it about a third of the way down the cake to form a branch. Frost cake, swirling the icing with a fork to make a bark pattern. Be sure to give it a knot.

Garnish sides of the cake with sprigs of fresh cedar. Plant the red candle in the top and serve. Serves 10.

COOK'S NOTE: I usually cover the unfrosted log and freeze it until a few hours before I need it.

CARROT PUDDING WITH TWO SAUCES

Old-time prairie cooks perfected this hefty steamed pudding, lavishing on it every spare raisin and carefully hoarded bit of glazed fruit they could muster. It's a lovely pud for our magnificently brisk winters, and it belongs as firmly to the Canadian Christmas tradition as did the plum pudding to the English.

1 cup	chopped suet	250 mL
1 cup	raisins	250 mL
1 cup	glazed fruit and peel	250 mL
2 cups	carrot, grated	500 mL
3/4 cup	brown sugar	175 mL
1/4 cup	molasses	50 mL
2 cups	flour, sifted	500 mL
1 tsp	cinnamon	5 mL
1/2 tsp each	cloves and nutmeg	2 mL each
1 tsp	baking soda	5 mL
1 tsp	salt	5 mL

❖ Stir suet, fruit and carrots together. Add sugar and molasses. Sift together flour, spices, baking soda and salt, and add to wet mixture. Beat well by hand. Spoon into a buttered, floured 4 cup (1 L) pudding mold, packing firmly. Cover with the lid or a well-buttered double thickness of foil secured with an elastic band.

Place the mold in a large roaster or Dutch oven, and pour boiling water halfway up the side of the mold. Bring water to a boil and turn down to simmer. Steam pudding about 4 hours or until it tests done. Serve hot. Some cooks flame their Christmas puds, but this is a buffet, so serve it with a sauceboat of Hot Rum Sauce and a dish of Brandied Hard Sauce.

This pudding keeps well in the fridge and freezes beautifully. Reheat in the microwave or by steaming 1 hour. Serves 10.

HOT RUM SAUCE

If you aren't fond of rum, use a plain brown sugar sauce (see Hot Butterscotch Sauce, January menu). Present this in a sauceboat or pitcher for easier service.

1 cup	brown sugar	250 mL
3/4 cup	corn syrup	175 mL
1/4 cup	butter	50 mL
1/4 cup	water	50 mL
1 to 2 tsp	rum extract	5 to 10 mL

❖ Put all ingredients except extract in a medium saucepan. Bring to a boil. Reduce heat to medium and cook until syrup forms a soft ball in a cold water test. Remove from heat and stir in rum extract. Serve hot. Makes 2 1/2 cups (600 mL)

COOK'S NOTE: If you'd rather use real rum, 1/4 cup (50 mL) is about right, though an extra drop or two won't hurt. Sauce keeps well in fridge and can be reheated to serve.

BRANDIED HARD SAUCE

1/2 cup	butter	125 mL
1 1/2 cups	sifted brown sugar	375 mL
1 tsp	vanilla	5 mL
2 tbsp	brandy	30 mL

❖ With a small electric mixer, whip butter until smooth. Add sifted sugar and beat well. Add vanilla and brandy, and beat until blended and smooth. Makes about 2 cups.

WHITE CHOCOLATE CHEESECAKE

This foolproof recipe is from the Baker's Chocolate people, and I cannot improve on perfection.

2	8 oz (250 g) pkgs cream cheese, softened	2
1/3 cup	sugar	75 mL
1 tsp	lemon juice	5 mL
6	squares white chocolate, melted	6
3/4 cup	sour cream	175 mL
2	large eggs	2
1 tsp	vanilla	5 mL
1 cup	sour cream	250 mL
2 tbsp	sugar	30 mL
	frosted cranberries for garnish	

❖   Preheat oven to 450 F (230 C).

Beat together cream cheese, sugar and lemon juice until blended and smooth. Add chocolate, sour cream, eggs and vanilla. Beat until well combined. Pour batter in a lightly greased 8 1/2 inch (22 cm) springform pan and smooth top. Bake 10 minutes. Reduce heat to 250 F (120 C) and bake 30 to 35 minutes longer.

For topping, combine sour cream and sugar. Spread over cheesecake. Bake 5 minutes more. Run a sharp knife around sides and let cool completely before removing sides. Refrigerate at least 5 hours or overnight. Garnish with frosted cranberries.

COOK'S NOTE: To frost berries, lightly whip an egg white with a fork. Roll fresh berries in egg white, then in granulated sugar. Let dry on waxed paper.

INDEX

INDEX